CULTURAL CHINESE

Cultural Chinese

READINGS IN ART, LITERATURE, AND HISTORY

文化中文

Zu-yan Chen and Hong Zhang

GEORGETOWN UNIVERSITY PRESS

Washington, D.C.

Georgetown University Press,
Washington, D.C. www.press.georgetown.edu

Library of Congress Cataloging-in-Publication Data
Chen, Zu-yan.
Cultural Chinese : readings in art, literature, and history /
Zu-yan Chen, Hong Zhang.
p. cm.
Includes bibliographical references and indexes.
ISBN 978-1-58901-882-2 (pbk. : alk. paper)
1. Chinese language—Readers. 2. Chinese language—Textbooks
for foreign speakers—English. I. Zhang, Hong. II. Title.
PL1117.C3748 2011
495.1′86421—dc22
2011016164

18 17 16 15 14 13 12   9 8 7 6 5 4 3 2
First printing

Printed in the United States of America

CONTENTS

PREFACE

SCENE 1: A Chinese-language teacher is having dinner with her students in a local Chinese restaurant. The teacher introduces the dishes: "This is *mapo doufu* and that is *gongbao jiding*."

SCENE 2: "Students, we will watch a video clip of Beijing opera for the rest of today's class." Students cheer as the teacher talks about face painting and other special characteristics of Beijing opera.

These scenes, so familiar to Chinese-language educators, demonstrate teachers' admirable efforts to stimulate student interest in Chinese language and culture. However, if these exciting activities are not supported by a curriculum with excellent cultural pedagogy, they may create the impression that culture in language learning is merely a bonus or hors d'oeuvre, an expendable fifth skill tacked on to the teaching of speaking, listening, reading, and writing. Experienced teachers and mature students should also raise such questions as What more should students learn about Chinese culture beyond spicy *mapo doufu* and the striking face painting and costuming of Beijing opera? How can we move from *incorporating* cultural activities to *integrating* cultural knowledge in the language curriculum? Can we provide advanced students with a course focusing on both linguistic and cultural competencies? *Cultural Chinese* attempts to provide answers to these operative questions as a textbook with a new approach to cultural integration and immersion.

This approach distinguishes itself by treating the exquisite connection between language and culture in a systematic and structured manner. Admittedly, Chinese-language education has always contained a cultural dimension, but language and culture often blend in relatively divergent ways. At the elementary and intermediate levels, students learn Chinese behavioral patterns and lifestyles; everyday language is tinged with cultural bits and pieces. Advanced textbooks often endow the study of language with a social hue, dealing with societal development and issues in China such as housing and employment. Culture, however, is often seen merely as information conveyed by the language, and not as a feature of language itself; cultural awareness becomes a separate educational objective from language. Instead of taking culture as a set of behavioral practices or social conditions, *Cultural*

Chinese seeks to identify and lend insights into the very fabric of Chinese culture that governs personal behavior and directs social dynamics.

In this book, then, culture assumes a unitary relationship with language and becomes the very core of language learning, by transitioning from context into text. Each of the nine lessons features a distinctive topic of Chinese culture, which serves as an important portal to Chinese perceptions and perspectives. The topic of each chapter is illustrated by three texts: the main text begins with a brief introduction of the topic, and is followed by two historical or mythological stories that bring to the fore certain elements of Chinese culture. An additional ministory 小故事 challenges students' abilities in cultural interpretation. The twenty-seven stories herein are ones with which every educated Chinese person is familiar. A section on knowledge 小知识 adds interesting information to the main text, equipping students with basic references of Chinese culture, from the Four Treasures of the Study 文房四宝 to the Four Books and Five Classics 四书五经 of Confucianism. Together, the three texts allow learners to increase their knowledge of the people's way of life, values, and attitudes, and how these manifest themselves or are couched in linguistic forms. The exercises are also intertwined with facets of culture. Questions often include analyses of the cultural implications of linguistic choices and show that culture has come to color language in many and varied ways. As a whole, *Cultural Chinese* aims at shedding light on the inner cohesion of language and cultural pedagogy while enriching and giving deeper meaning to what is dubbed "communicative competence."

We would like to thank Chen Xuelun, a renowned artist in Shanghai and a life-long friend of ours, for the excellent illustrations he made for this book. With his profound knowledge of Chinese culture and superior artistic talent, he has created nine works of art that will establish lively and memorable images in the reader's mind. We are especially pleased that our friendship with Xuelun has not only endured across decades and thousands of miles, but also flourished with our collaboration on this project.

USER'S GUIDE

1. This textbook can be used for courses in advanced Chinese or Chinese culture.

2. Each lesson comprises three major parts: texts, language points, and exercises. The first part consists of three texts: a main text, a ministory 小故事, and a knowledge 小知识 section. Accordingly, there are three vocabulary lists. Language points provide practice using words, sentence patterns, and idioms. The ten-plus sections of exercises provide an ample source of classroom practice and homework assignments.

3. When doing certain exercises, students may need to use a Chinese dictionary (hard copy or online). In those exercises requiring translation from Chinese into English 中译英, interpretations are supplied only for those words likely to confuse students.

4. English translations of the texts are included in the appendix.

5. Sections of the exercises—including debate, composition, storytelling, and topical research—require students to do research on the Internet. These research projects, although brief in nature and limited in scope, will challenge students to check information and resources in Chinese and English, and to report their findings in Chinese.

CALLIGRAPHY 书法

"Preface to the *Orchid Pavilion*" and
"The Pagoda of Many Treasures"
《兰亭序》与《多宝塔》

汉字的书写艺术源远流长。从商朝的甲骨文算起，已经有三千五百多年的历史。周朝用金文，秦朝用篆书，汉朝用隶书。到晋朝，楷书、草书和行书都已形成。我们现在写的，基本上是楷书。在书法作品中，常常能看到隶书、草书和行书。刻图章时，用篆书的还很多。

中国历史上有很多杰出的书法家。晋朝的王羲之被后世称为"书圣"。他年轻时练字十分刻苦。他家旁边有个池塘，他常在那儿洗毛笔和砚台。时间长了，池水都黑了。那个池塘就成了有名的"墨池"。

王羲之的作品中最著名的是《兰亭序》。有一次，王羲之和朋友们在浙江的兰亭聚会，饮酒赋诗。王羲之当场写了《兰亭序》。这篇书法如行云流水，清新自然。其中有二十多个"之"字，竟然没有一个相同的。王羲之后来把《兰亭序》又写了很多遍，但都不如原作，就把这幅字作为传家宝。《兰亭序》被后世称为"天下第一行书"。

王羲之身后差不多四百年，唐朝的颜真卿又开创了一个书法艺术的新时代。他三岁时父亲去世，家里很穷，连纸笔都买不起，只能用扫帚蘸着黄泥浆在墙上练字。他写过一首《劝学》诗："三更灯火五更鸡，正是男儿读书时。黑发不知勤学早，白首方悔读书迟。"这不就是他自己勤学苦练的写照吗？

那时，唐朝有很多叛乱，颜真卿英勇地跟叛军作战。七十五岁时，颜真卿去一支叛军中劝降。到了那里，一千多名叛军围住他，拔出刀对着他，但颜真卿面不改色。后来，叛军又对他进行长期的威胁利诱，但颜真卿始终坚贞不屈。结果，叛军把他杀死了。

　　后人说颜真卿"明若日月、坚若金石"的人格造就了他卓越的书法艺术。颜真卿的楷书每个字都厚实有力。他的书法代表作有《多宝塔碑》等。中国有句话叫"字如其人"，在颜真卿的身上得到了最好的体现。

词汇一 VOCABULARY I

书法	書法	shūfǎ	calligraphy
序		xù	preface
宝	寶	bǎo	treasure
塔		tǎ	pagoda
源远流长	源遠流長	yuányuǎn liúcháng	distant source and long stream (a metaphor for something of long standing)
形成		xíngchéng	to form
甲骨文		jiǎgǔwén	oracle bone script (inscriptions on tortoise shells or animal bones)
金文		jīnwén	inscriptions on bronze
篆书	篆書	zhuànshū	seal script
基本上		jīběnshàng	basically
隶书	隸書	lìshū	clerical script
楷书	楷書	kǎishū	regular script
草书	草書	cǎoshū	cursive script
行书	行書	xíngshū	running script
作品		zuòpǐn	works (of art and literature)
刻		kè	to carve
图章	圖章	túzhāng	seal, stamp
杰出	傑出	jiéchū	outstanding, excellent
后世	後世	hòushì	later generations
称为	稱爲	chēngwéi	to be called
圣	聖	shèng	sage
刻苦		kèkǔ	hardworking, painstaking
池塘		chítáng	pond
毛笔	毛筆	máobǐ	writing brush

砚台	硯臺	yàntai	inkstone
墨		mò	ink, inkstick
著名		zhùmíng	famous
聚会	聚會	jùhuì	gathering, party
赋诗	賦詩	fùshī	to compose poems
当场	當場	dāngchǎng	on the spot
如		rú	像
行云	行雲	xíngyún	floating clouds
清新		qīngxīn	fresh, refreshing
其中		qízhōng	among them
之		zhī	的
竟然		jìngrán	surprisingly
原作		yuánzuò	original work
幅		fú	measure word for cloth, pictures, scrolls, etc.
传家宝	傳家寶	chuánjiābǎo	heirloom
天下		tiānxià	under the heavens; world, country
身后	身後	shēnhòu	after one's death
开创	開創	kāichuàng	to open, to create
时代	時代	shídài	age, era
扫帚	掃帚	sàozhǒu	broom
蘸		zhàn	to dip in
墙	墙	qiáng	wall
泥浆		níjiāng	slop, soft mud
劝	勸	quàn	to persuade, to urge
更	更	gēng	one of the five two-hour periods into which the night was divided in ancient times
灯火	燈火	dēnghuǒ	lights
正		zhèng	exactly
男儿	男兒	nán'ér	男人
勤		qín	diligent
白首		báishǒu	white-haired, aged
方		fāng	才
悔		huǐ	to regret

迟	遲	chí	晚
写照	寫照	xiězhào	portrait, depiction
叛乱	叛亂	pànluàn	rebellion
英勇		yīngyǒng	heroic, brave
作战	作戰	zuòzhàn	to fight, to fight a battle
支		zhī	measure word for army units, etc.
降	降	xiáng	to surrender
围	圍	wéi	to surround
拔		bá	to draw (a sword)
面不改色		miàn bù gǎisè	to keep one's composure
利诱	利誘	lìyòu	to tempt with material gain
利		lì	profit
诱	誘	yòu	to tempt
始终	始終	shǐzhōng	from beginning to end, for all time
坚贞不屈	堅貞不屈	jiānzhēn bùqū	to remain faithful and unyielding
若		ruò	像
人格		réngé	personality, moral quality
造就		zàojìu	to bring up, to foster
卓越		zhuóyuè	outstanding, excellent
厚实	厚實	hòushí	deep and solid
碑		bēi	stele, tombstone
其		qí	his, her, its, their
体现		tǐxiàn	manifestation, reflection, expression

专名一 PROPER NAMES I

浙江		Zhèjiāng	Zhejiang Province
兰亭	蘭亭	Lántíng	Orchid Pavilion, in Shaoxing 绍兴 City, Zhejiang Province
商朝		Shāngcháo	Shang dynasty (1600–1046 BCE)
周朝		Zhōucháo	Zhou dynasty (1046–256 BCE)
秦朝		Qíncháo	Qin dynasty (221–206 BCE)
汉朝	漢朝	Hàncháo	Han dynasty (202 BCE–220 CE)

晋朝	Jìncháo	Jin dynasty (265-420)
王羲之	Wáng Xīzhī	Jin calligrapher (321-379)
颜真卿	Yán Zhēnqīng	Tang calligrapher and statesman (708-784)
唐朝	Tángcháo	Tang dynasty (618-907)

小故事 Ministory
Eighteen Vats of Water 十八缸水

王献之是王羲之的第七个儿子，从小就跟父亲学书法。有一次，小献之正在聚精会神地练字，王羲之悄悄走到他背后，突然伸手去抽献之手中的毛笔。献之握笔很牢，没被抽掉。父亲很高兴，称赞道："这个孩子将来会有出息。"

一天，小献之问父亲："我再写三年就行了吧？"父亲摇摇头。"五年总行了吧？"父亲又摇摇头。献之急了："那您说究竟要多长时间?""你要记住，写完院子里这十八缸水，你的字才写得好。"

王献之又苦练了五年。他把一大堆写好的字给父亲看，希望听到几句表扬的话。谁知，王羲之边看边摇头。看到一个"大"字，父亲点点头，随手在"大"字下加了一点，变成一个"太"字。

小献之又把全部习字抱给母亲看，说："我又练了五年，并且完全是按照父亲的字练的。您仔细看看，我和父亲的字还有什么不同?"母亲认真地看了三天，然后指着王羲之在"大"字下加的那个点儿，叹了口气说："吾儿磨尽三缸水，惟有一点像羲之。"

献之听后很受启发，又继续苦练，终于写完了十八缸水。功夫不负有心人，王献之也成了大书法家，和他父亲齐名，被人们并称为"二王"。

词汇二 VOCABULARY II

聚精会神	聚精會神	jùjīng huìshén	to focus one's attention on, to be engrossed in
聚		jù	to assemble, to gather
悄悄		qiāoqiāo	quietly
伸手		shēnshǒu	to hold out one's hand
抽		chōu	to remove from in between, to draw
牢		láo	firm
称赞	稱讚	chēngzàn	to praise
道		dào	说
出息		chūxi	bright future
究竟		jiūjìng	actually, after all
缸		gāng	vat
堆		duī	pile, stack, heap
表扬	表揚	biǎoyáng	to commend
随手	隨手	suíshǒu	conveniently, without extra trouble
犬		quǎn	狗, dog
并且	並且	bìngqiě	而且
按照		ànzhào	according to
叹	嘆	tàn	to sigh
吾		wú	我
磨		mó	to grind
尽	盡	jìn	exhausted
惟有		wéiyǒu	只有
受		shòu	to receive
启发	啓發	qǐfā	enlightenment
继续	繼續	jìxù	to continue
终于	終于	zhōngyú	finally, eventually
功夫		gōngfu	time, effort
负	負	fù	to let down, to disappoint
齐名	齊名	qímíng	to be equally famous
并称	並稱	bìngchēng	to be named together and equivalently

专名二 PROPER NAMES II

王献之　王獻之　Wáng Xiànzhī　Jin calligrapher (344–386)

小知识 Knowledge
Major Dynasties 主要朝代

中国历史上大大小小的朝代很多。其中有十个主要的朝代。

周朝	前1046–前256
秦朝	前221–前206
汉朝	前202–220
六朝	221–589
隋朝	581–617
唐朝	618–907
宋朝	960–1279
元朝	1271–1368
明朝	1368–1644
清朝	1644–1911

　　周朝是最长的一个朝代，将近八百年。秦朝和隋朝都很短，但都统一了中国，并建立了一些重要的制度。汉朝是一个影响深远的朝代，从汉族、汉语等词汇中就能看到。六朝是六个朝代的集合体。唐、宋、元、明、清经常连在一起说，是最后五个重要的朝代。

词汇三 VOCABULARY III

朝代		cháodài	dynasty
将近	將近	jiāngjìn	nearly, almost
统一	統一	tóngyī	to unify
制度		zhìdù	rules, regulations, system
影响深远	影響深遠	yǐngxiǎng shēnyuǎn	profound influence
集合体	集合體	jíhétǐ	collection

专名三 PROPER NAMES III

隋朝	Suícháo	Sui dynasty (581–618)
宋朝	Sòngcháo	Song dynasty (960–1276)
元朝	Yuáncháo	Yuan dynasty (1271–1368)
明朝	Míngcháo	Ming dynasty (1368–1644)
清朝	Qīngcháo	Qing dynasty (1636–1911)

语言点 Language Points

一、词语 WORDS

1. 其中 among them, of them

   【课文】其中有二十多个"之"字，竟然无一相同。

   【例句】今天我跟他打了五局乒乓球，其中三局我没赢，还有两局他没输。

   I played five games of ping-pong with him today. I didn't win three of them and he didn't lose the other two.

2. 竟然 surprisingly

   【课文】其中有二十多个"之"字，竟然无一相同。

   【例句】她只学了两年钢琴，竟然能弹贝多芬的曲子了，真了不起！

   She has studied piano for only two years; surprisingly, she can play pieces by Beethoven — it's really amazing!

3. 不如 not as good as

   【课文】王羲之后来把《兰亭序》又写了很多遍，但都不如原作。

   【例句】这双皮鞋不如那双漂亮，可是穿着比较舒服，我应该买哪一双呢？

   This pair of shoes is not as pretty as that pair, but it's more comfortable. Which should I buy?

4. 正 exactly

   【课文】三更灯火五更鸡，正是男儿读书时。

   【例句】经济发展正是我们大家所关心的问题。

   Economic development is exactly the issue all of us are concerned with.

5. 造就 to bring up, to foster

【课文】颜真卿"明若日月，坚若金石"的人格造就了他卓越的书法艺术。

【例句】网络时代造就了一大批电子商务企业家。

The Internet age created a large number of e-business entrepreneurs.

6. 究竟 actually, after all

【课文】那您说究竟要多长时间？

【例句】我已经大四了，可我还不知道将来究竟要做什么。

I am already a college senior, but I still don't know what I am actually going to do in the future.

7. 终于 finally, eventually

【课文】献之听完后很受启发，又继续苦练，终于写完了十八缸水。

【例句】我终于明白了小王为什么这么用功地学习中文，原来他打算毕业后去中国工作。

I finally understand why Xiao Wang works so hard at studying Chinese. It turns out that he plans to work in China after graduation.

二、句型 SENTENCE PATTERNS

1. 从……算起 counting from

【课文】从商朝的甲骨文算起，已经有三千五百多年的历史。

【例句】从小学算起，一直到大学毕业，父母在孩子身上得花多少钱啊。

From elementary school up through college graduation, parents must spend so much money on their children!

2. 被……称为 to be called by

【课文】晋朝的王羲之被后世称为"书圣"。

【例句】人人都爱唱他的歌，所以他被称为"流行歌曲之王"。

Everyone likes to sing his songs; that's why he is called the "King of Popular Song."

3. 连……都 even

【课文】他三岁时父亲去世，家里很穷，连纸笔都买不起。

【例句】爷爷连电子邮件都不会打，你还叫他写博客？别开玩笑了。

Grandpa doesn't even know how to write e-mails, but you want to ask him to write a blog? Don't be silly.

4. 对……进行 to take action toward a certain person or on a certain subject

【课文】后来，叛军又对他进行长期的威胁利诱。

【例句】李教授对这个数学难题进行了长期的研究，终于写出了一篇出色的论文。

Professor Li researched this difficult math problem for a long time and ultimately wrote an outstanding paper.

5. 从……看到 to see from a certain perspective

【课文】汉朝是一个影响深远的朝代，从汉族、汉语等词汇中就能看到。

【例句】从上海城市建设的飞快发展我们就能看到中国这几年的巨大变化。

By observing the rapid development of the city of Shanghai, we can see huge changes in China over several years.

三、成语 IDIOMS

1. 源远流长 distant source and long stream

【课文】汉字的书写艺术源远流长。

【例句】我们俩的友谊可以说是源远流长了——我们从小学到大学一直是同学。

The friendship between the two of us can be said to have a distant source and long stream—we have been classmates from elementary school through college.

2. 勤学苦练 to study industriously and practice painstakingly

【课文】这正是他自己勤学苦练的写照。

【例句】你要知道那个书法家是怎么勤学苦练的吗？你去看看他那一屋子用坏的毛笔吧。

Would you like to know how industrious that calligrapher is? Go take a look at the roomful of brushes he's worn out.

3. 面不改色 to keep one's composure

　　【课文】叛军拔出刀对着他，但颜真卿面不改色。

　　【例句】听到这个坏消息，一屋子的人都大惊失色，只有他一
　　　　　 个人面不改色。

　　　　Having heard this bad news, everyone in the room went pale with fear;
　　　　only he kept his composure.

4. 聚精会神 to focus one's attention on, to be engrossed in

　　【课文】小献之正在聚精会神地练字，王羲之悄悄走到他背
　　　　　 后。

　　【例句】爸爸正在聚精会神地写文章呢，我们别进去打扰他。

　　　　Dad is engrossed in writing an article; let's not go in and disturb him.

练习 Exercises

一、填名词

Fill in the blanks with appropriate nouns to form adjective-noun phrases.

1. 杰出的 ＿＿＿ ＿＿＿
2. 刻苦的 ＿＿＿ ＿＿＿
3. 著名的 ＿＿＿ ＿＿＿
4. 清新的 ＿＿＿ ＿＿＿
5. 英勇的 ＿＿＿ ＿＿＿
6. 卓越的 ＿＿＿ ＿＿＿
7. 厚实的 ＿＿＿ ＿＿＿
8. 认真的 ＿＿＿ ＿＿＿

二、选词填空

Fill in the blanks using the words provided.

（其中、竟然、不如、正是、造就、究竟、终于）

1. 这个有名的大学 ＿＿＿＿ 了很多世界有名的科学家。
2. 我们学校有很多外国留学生，＿＿＿＿ 三分之一是从中国来
　　的。
3. 我今天才知道你的女朋友 ＿＿＿＿ 是我的表姐！
4. 我今天 ＿＿＿＿ 登上了长城，实现了我多年的愿望。

5. 苏州虽然 _________ 上海那么繁华，但有很多漂亮的园林，也是
很好玩的啊。
6. 你今天一直不说话，_________ 是为了什么啊？
7. 我说的 _________ 那位教授，他不但教书教得好，而且人也好。

三、用句型造句

Compose sentences using the sentence patterns below.
1. 从……算起
2. 被……称为
3. 连……都
4. 对……进行
5. 从……看到

四、用本课的成语改写句子

Rewrite each sentence using idioms you have learned in this lesson.
1. 他做什么事都三心二意的，只有在打短信的时候思想才能集
中。
2. 我真佩服那位运动员，还有两分就要输了，却没有一点紧张的
样子。
3. 这个故事在周朝就有了，有很长的历史了。
4. 古今中外哪个艺术家的成功不是靠天才加上努力？

五、选择题

Choose the correct word or phrase to complete each sentence.
1.王羲之的《兰亭序》是 _________。
　　a. 隶书　　b. 行书
　　c. 楷书　　d. 草书

2.颜真卿连纸笔都买不起，只能用 _________ 蘸着黄泥浆在墙上练
字。
　　a. 树枝　　b. 铅笔
　　c. 手指　　d. 扫帚

3. ＿＿＿＿＿＿＿ 方悔读书迟。
　　a. 三更　　b. 五更
　　c. 黑发　　d. 白首

4. 这个孩子将来会有 ＿＿＿＿＿＿＿。
　　a. 出息　　b. 出路
　　c. 出名　　d. 出头

5. 中国有句话叫"字如其人"，在颜真卿的身上得到了最好的
　　＿＿＿＿＿＿＿。
　　a. 发现　　b. 出现
　　c. 体现　　d. 表现

6. ＿＿＿＿＿＿＿ 朝是最长的一个朝代，将近八百年。
　　a. 周　　　b. 汉
　　c. 唐　　　d. 明

六、改错

Correct the sentences below.

1. 我们现在写的，基本上是草书。
2. 刻图章时，用隶书的还很多。
3. 王羲之后来把《兰亭序》又写了很多遍，越写越好。
4. 三更灯火五更鸡，正是男儿睡觉时。
5. 颜真卿七十五岁时奉皇帝的命令去跟叛军作战。
6. 王献之把一大堆写好的字给父亲看，希望听到几句表扬的话。王羲之边看边点头。
7. 王羲之随手在"大"字上加了一点，变成一个"犬"字。
8. 王献之的母亲叹了口气说："吾儿磨尽三缸水，没有一点像羲之。"

七、回答问题

Answer the questions below.

1. 汉字的书写艺术有多长的历史？
2. 商朝时，字是写在什么东西上的？
3. 《兰亭序》是在怎么样的情况下写的？
4. 《兰亭序》被后世称为什么？

5. 颜真卿小时候是怎么勤学苦练的？
6. 颜真卿是怎么死的？
7. 颜真卿的楷书有什么特点？
8. 颜字表现出他什么样的人格？
9. 王羲之为什么称赞王献之有出息？
10. 王羲之跟王献之说什么时候才能把字写好？
11. 隋朝和秦朝有什么相似的地方？
12. 你怎么知道汉朝是个影响深远的朝代？
13. 中国最后五个重要的朝代是什么？

八、英译中

Translate the passages below into Chinese.

1. In the spring of 352, Wang Xizhi invited forty-one friends to a party at the Orchid Pavilion, where they drank and composed poems. By the end of the day, thirty-seven poems had been written by twenty-five scholars, and Wang Xizhi wrote a preface to their poems on the spot. Although later Wang Xizhi tried many times to reproduce the work, he was never able to match the quality of the original. "Preface to the *Orchid Pavilion*" has been revered by generations of calligraphers as the finest running script under the heavens.

2. It is said that Wang Xizhi had a special fondness for geese. Once, Wang Xizhi saw a flock of geese in a pond and really took a fancy to them. Therefore, he wrote a work of calligraphy in exchange for a goose. Today, there is a goose pond in the Orchid Pavilion Park in Shaoxing. Inscribed on the stone tablet are two Chinese characters: 鹅池, of which the first is said to have been written by Wang Xizhi and the second by his youngest son, Wang Xianzhi.

3. Once, Wang Xizhi passed by a stone bridge in Shaoxing. He saw an old woman selling bamboo fans, but it seemed nobody was interested in them. Out of his desire to help the poor woman, Wang Xizhi wrote a few words on each of her fans. On hearing that the fans bore the inscriptions of Wang Xizhi, people clamored to buy them. In present-day Shaoxing, there is an arched stone bridge 石拱桥 that is believed to be the very one where Wang Xizhi inscribed the fans; it is called the "Fan-inscribing Bridge" 题扇桥.

九、中译英

Translate the passages below into English.

1. 入木三分①

   绍兴城里有一家店铺，想换个新的招牌。他们找来一块上面写着字的好木板。老板叫人把木板上的毛笔字洗去，好写新的内容。哪知擦洗了半天，虽然把墨洗掉了，但是字迹还印刻在木板上，依然清晰可见。人们惊讶了：这样有力的字是谁写的啊？他们请了一位懂得书法的老先生来看。老先生一看，立即惊叫起来："这是大书法家王羲之的笔迹啊！他的书法真是入木三分啊！"

   【生词】① 分 a unit of length (= 1/3 of centimeter)

2. "退笔冢"和"铁门槛"①隋唐时代的著名书法家智永和尚，是王羲之的七世孙。他曾住在永欣寺楼上，刻苦学书三十年，写秃了无数的毛笔。他把秃笔都埋在一起，称为"退笔冢"。他亲手临写的《千字文》有八百多本，② 分别散在江南各寺庙里。"只要功夫深，铁杵磨成针"，智永终于成为当时著名的书法家。每天来求他写字的人络绎不绝，把他家的门槛都踏穿了，于是用铁皮包上，被人称为"铁门槛"。

   【生词】① 退 to retire from, to quit ② 千字文 *Thousand Character Reader,* a children's primer written in the sixth century

十、故事复述

Retell the following stories:

1. 王羲之 "墨池。"
2. 王羲之写《兰亭序》。
3. 颜真卿练字。
4. 颜真卿字如其人。
5. 十八缸水。

十一、课堂辩论

Debate the question posed below.

   【题目】练字能用扫帚吗？

【提示】正方：颜鲁公用扫帚蘸着黄泥浆在墙上练字的精神现在还要发扬。这是中国的艰苦奋斗、发愤图强的传统。反方：现代社会条件好了，这样的传统没有必要保存。再说，孔子也说过："工欲善其事，必先利其器。"练字就要用毛笔，而且要好的毛笔。

十二、作文

Write a short composition of approximately three hundred characters on the topic below.

【题目】写中文字的苦与乐【提示】你已经写了两年多中文字了，其中一定有苦也有乐。讲一个苦的故事和一个乐的故事。一定要有趣！

十三、专题研究

Research the following topics online and report to the class.

1. 【题目一】介绍一幅有名的书法作品。
2. 【题目二】字和画　　【提示】中国字最早是象形文字，每个字就像一幅画。举几个例子，做一点介绍。

十四、背诵

Recite the following from memory:

1. 颜真卿《劝学》诗。
2. 十个主要朝代的名字。

CHINESE PAINTING 国画

"Ink Plum Blossoms" and "Ink Bamboo"
《墨梅图》与《墨竹图》

　　中国传统绘画简称国画，可分为山水画、花鸟画和人物画等种类。国画要求诗、书、画的完美结合，所以很多画家也是诗人和书法家。此外，中国画家很重视所画的动物、植物的象征意义。比如，画家很喜欢画松树，这是因为孔子说过："岁寒然后知松柏之后凋也。"同样的，竹子四季常青，梅花不畏严寒，所以画家常常把松、竹、梅画在一起，叫做"岁寒三友"。

　　说到画梅，就会想起王冕。元代著名画家、诗人王冕出生在一个贫苦人家。他小时候一边给人放牛，一边念书。有一天，他把牛放在草地上，自己跑到附近的学校里去听学生读书。傍晚回来时，牛找不到了，结果被他父亲打了一顿。

　　长大后，王冕没有做官，而是以卖画为生。他在园子里种了一千多株梅树，自称"梅花屋主"。他在一幅《墨梅图》上题诗道："吾家洗砚池头树，个个花开淡墨痕。不要人夸好颜色，只留清气满乾坤。"第一、第二句描写梅花，第三、第四两句赞扬梅花的品格：它不想用鲜艳的色彩去吸引人，只愿散发一股清香，让它留在天地之间。这两句也是诗人的自我写照。

　　与梅花同属"岁寒三友"的竹子也为画家所喜爱。清朝的郑燮，字板桥，就以画竹著称。人们常用"胸有成竹"来形容他画竹技艺的高超。有一天，郑板桥生病躺在床上。他看见窗外的竹子在狂风暴雨中依然挺立。他马上从床上起来，画了一幅《墨竹图》，并在画上题诗道："咬定青山不放松，立根原在破岩中。千磨万击还坚劲，任尔东西南北风。"这首诗既说明竹子的处境，又歌颂竹子的精神。诗和画在一起，成为传世珍宝。

词汇一 VOCABULARY I

绘画	繪畫	huìhuà	painting
简称	簡稱	jiǎnchēng	abbreviated name or title
种类	種類	zhǒnglèi	kind, category
完美		wánměi	perfect
此外		cǐwài	besides, in addition
植物		zhíwù	plant, vegetable
寒		hán	冷
松		sōng	pine
柏		bǎi	cypress
凋		diāo	to wither
季		jì	season
青		qīng	greenish blue
畏		wèi	怕
严寒	嚴寒	yánhán	severe cold
贫苦	貧苦	pínkǔ	poor, poverty stricken
放牛		fàngniú	to herd water buffalo
傍晚		bàngwǎn	dusk
顿	頓	dùn	measure word for actions
官		guān	government official
株		zhū	measure word for trees and plants
淡		dàn	light (color)
痕		hén	mark, trace
夸	誇	kuā	to praise
满	滿	mǎn	full
乾坤		qiánkūn	天地, universe
描写	描寫	miáoxiě	to describe
品格		pǐngé	moral character
鲜艳	鮮豔	xiānyàn	brightly colored
色彩		sècǎi	color
吸引		xīyǐn	to attract
散发	散發	sànfā	to scatter, to disperse
股		gǔ	measure word for smells, etc.
香		xiāng	fragrance

与	與	yǔ	和
字		zì	style name
胸有成竹		xiōng yǒu chéngzhú	having painted bamboo in mind (a metaphor for having a ready plan)
成		chéng	completed, matured
形容		xíngróng	to describe
技艺	技藝	jìyì	skill, artistry
高超		gāochāo	superb, outstanding
狂风暴雨	狂風暴雨	kuángfēng bàoyǔ	fierce wind and torrential rain, violent storm
依然		yīrán	still, as usual
挺立		tǐnglì	to stand upright
题诗	題詩	tíshī	to inscribe a poem (on a painting, etc.)
咬		yǎo	to bite
定		dìng	firmly
放松	放鬆	fàngsōng	to loosen
根		gēn	root
破		pò	broken
岩		yán	rock
击	擊	jī	to strike, to beat
坚劲	堅勁	jiānjìng	strong
任		rèn	to let one act at will, no matter (how, what, etc.)
尔	爾	ěr	你
说明	説明	shuōmíng	to explain, to illustrate
处境	處境	chǔjìng	(unfavorable) situation
歌颂	歌頌	gēsòng	to sing praise
精神		jīngshén	spirit
传世	傳世	chuánshì	to be handed down from generation to generation
珍宝	珍寶	zhēnbǎo	treasure

专名一 PROPER NAMES I

孔子		Kǒngzǐ	Confucius (551–479 BCE)
王冕		Wáng Miǎn	Yuan painter (1287–1359)
郑燮	鄭燮	Zhèng Xiè	Qing painter (1693–1765)

小故事 Ministory
The Poet and the Thief 赋诗送贼

　　一天深夜，郑板桥躺在床上，忽见窗纸上映出一个人影。他想：不好，有小偷来了。我既打不过他，又不能让他偷东西。怎么办呢？想了一下，他就低声吟道："细雨蒙蒙夜沉沉，梁上君子进我门。"

　　这时，小偷已进屋，听到后吃了一惊。接着又听道："腹内诗书存千卷，床头金银无半文。"小偷心想：原来是个穷人，就不偷了。他转身出门，又听里面说："出门休惊黄尾犬。"小偷想，既然有狗，那我就翻墙出去吧。正要上墙，又听："越墙莫损兰花盆。"小偷一看，墙头真的有兰花一盆。这时，黄狗追出来咬住小偷。郑板桥出门，又念了两句诗："天寒不及披衣送，收拾雄心重做人。"

词汇二 VOCABULARY II

赋诗	賦	fùshī	to compose a poem
贼	賊	zéi	thief
映		yìng	to reflect, to show through
影		yǐng	shadow
过	過	guò	used after a verb plus 得 or 不 to indicate superiority or inferiority, success or failure, etc., such as in 打不過
吟		yín	to chant (poems)
细雨	細雨	xìyǔ	fine rain
蒙蒙	濛濛	méngméng	drizzly

夜沉沉		yè chénchén	deep in the night
梁上君子	樑上君子	liángshàng jūnzǐ	thief
梁	樑	liáng	roof beam
君子		jūnzǐ	gentleman
吃惊	吃驚	chījīng	to be startled
腹		fù	belly
存		cún	to exist
卷		juàn	volume
文		wén	measure word for ancient coins
休		xiū	不要
尾		wěi	tail
翻		fān	to cross, to get over, to climb over
墙	牆	qiáng	wall
越	越	yuè	to cross, to get over
莫		mò	不要
损	損	sǔn	to damage
兰花	蘭花	lánhuā	orchid
（來）不及		(lái) bùjí	not enough time (to do something)
披		pī	to drape over one's shoulders
收拾		shōushi	to pick up
雄心		xióngxīn	lofty aspiration
重		chóng	anew, afresh
做人		zuòrén	to be a person of integrity

小知识 Knowledge

Four Treasures of the Study 文房四宝

　　文房是指古时候文人的书房，文房四宝是对笔、墨、纸、砚四种写字作画的文具的统称。中国古代文人是离不开这四件宝贝的。

　　笔是毛笔。因为书法上依照字体大小分大楷、中楷和小楷，毛笔也可分为大楷笔、中楷笔和小楷笔。

墨也有很多讲究。写字的时候，墨要磨得又浓又匀才好。

纸是中国古代四大发明之一，从汉代起就造纸了。有一种宣纸最适合书画。

砚，也叫砚台。有的砚台是选用很好的石头做的，又有精美的雕刻，所以也是工艺品。

当然，文房四宝对书画家是很重要的，但颜真卿用扫帚蘸着黄泥浆在墙上练字的精神也不能忘记啊。

词汇三 VOCABULARY III

文房		wénfáng	书房
文人		wénrén	man of letters, scholar
文具		wénjù	stationery
统称	統稱	tǒngchēng	collective name, general designation
宝贝	寶貝	bǎobèi	treasure
依照		yīzhào	按照
字体	字體	zìtǐ	style of calligraphy
讲究	講究	jiǎngjiu	to be particular about, to pay attention to, to stress
浓	濃	nóng	thick, dense, heavy
匀		yún	even
发明	發明	fāmíng	invention
宣纸	宣紙	xuānzhǐ	*Xuan* paper
精美		jīngměi	exquisite
雕刻		diāokè	carved work
工艺品	工藝品	gōngyìpǐn	a work of handicraft

语言点 Language Points

一、词语 WORDS

1. 此外 besides, in addition

【课文】此外，中国画家很重视所画的动物、植物的象征意义。

【例句】今天我们去夫子庙主要是参观古迹，此外，也要尝尝附近街上各种有名的小吃。

We will see mainly historical sites when we visit the Confucius Temple today. In addition, we will try different snacks for which the area streets are famous.

2. 比如 for example

【课文】此外，中国画家很重视所画的动物、植物的象征意义。比如，画家很喜欢画松树，这是因为孔子说过："岁寒然后知松柏之后凋也。"

【例句】我很喜欢吃中国菜，比如，麻婆豆腐、左宗鸡和红烧牛肉。

I like Chinese dishes such as *mapo doufu,* General Zuo's chicken, and beef with soy sauce.

3. 结果 as a result

【课文】傍晚回来时，牛找不到了，结果被他父亲打了一顿。

【例句】丽丽要漂亮，下雪天还穿短裙，结果感冒了。

Lili likes to look pretty and wears short skirts even on snowy days. As a result, she caught a cold.

4. 吸引 to attract

【课文】它不想用鲜艳的色彩去吸引人，只愿散发一股清香，让它留在天地之间。

【例句】他的这篇文章写得非常有趣，一上网就吸引了很多眼球。

This article of his is very interesting. As soon as it was posted online, it caught many people's eyes.

5. 依然 still, as usual

【课文】他看见窗外的竹子在狂风暴雨中，依然挺立。

【例句】昨晚一场大雨把很多花都打坏了，只有那朵玫瑰花依然张开着笑脸。

A rainstorm last night damaged many flowers; only that rose still blooms with its smiling face.

6. 讲究 to be particular about, to pay attention to, to stress

【课文】墨也有很多讲究。

【例句】写汉字讲究笔划顺序，不能随便。

When writing Chinese characters, one needs to pay attention to stroke order and not write carelessly.

二、 句型 SENTENCE PATTERNS

1. 所 V 的 (emphasizing object of the verb)

【课文】中国画家很重视所画的动物、植物的象征意义。

【例句】父母所做的都是为了孩子，孩子所做的又是为了谁呢？

Everything parents do is for their children, but for whom do children act?

2. 以 …… 为生 to live on (certain resources)

【课文】长大后，王冕没有做官，而是以卖画为生。

【例句】那位画家很可怜，每天在街上以给人画像为生。

That painter is very pathetic. He makes a living by drawing portraits for people on the streets every day.

3. 为 …… 所（喜爱）to be (loved [or other verbs]) by

【课文】与梅花同属"岁寒三友"的竹子也为画家所喜爱。

【例句】你看那个大熊猫吃竹子的样子多可爱，难怪它们为世人所喜爱。

See how cute that giant panda looks as he eats bamboo. No wonder they are loved by people all over the world.

4. 既 …… 又 …… both … and …, neither … nor …

【课文】我既打不过他，又不能让他偷东西。

【例句】我现在既没钱又没时间，还是以后再去欧洲旅行吧。

I have neither time nor money now. We'd better travel to Europe later on.

5. 既然 …… 就 since

【课文】小偷想，既然有狗，那我就翻墙出去吧。

【例句】你既然不喜欢学商业，那就换一个专业吧，还来得及。

Since you don't like studying business, you should change your major. You still have time.

6. V + 不过 to have no match

【课文】我既打不过他，又不能让他偷东西。

【例句】小唐下棋可厉害啦，我们班谁都下不过他。

Xiao Tang plays chess extremely well. Nobody in our class can match him.

三、成语 IDIOMS

1. 四季常青 evergreen

  【课文】同样的，竹子四季常青，梅花不畏严寒，所以画家常常把松、竹、梅画在一起，叫做"岁寒三友"。

  【例句】我喜欢四季常青的植物，因为秋天不用扫落叶。

  I like evergreen plants because I don't want to rake fallen leaves in the autumn.

2. 胸有成竹 having painted bamboo in mind (a metaphor for having a ready plan)

  【课文】人们常用"胸有成竹"来形容他画竹技艺的高超。

  【例句】明天的考试我胸有成竹，考不到一百分我请你吃饭。

  I am completely ready for tomorrow's exam. If I do not get 100 percent, I will take you out to dinner.

3. 狂风暴雨 fierce wind and torrential rain, violent storm

  【课文】他看见窗外的竹子在狂风暴雨中，依然挺立。

  【例句】天气预报说今天要有狂风暴雨，怎么现在还是风和日丽呢？

  The weather forecast said that there will be a violent storm today. How come it is still so nice out now?

4. 传世珍宝 treasures handed down from older generations

  【课文】诗和画在一起，成为传世珍宝。

  【例句】小宋说他写毛笔字用的那个破砚台是传世珍宝，你信不信？

  Xiao Song said that the shabby inkstone he uses for brush writing is a treasure passed down from ancient times. Do you believe that?

练习 Exercises

一、填名词

Fill in the blanks with appropriate nouns to form adjective-noun phrases.

1. 完美的 _____ _____
2. 严寒的 _____ _____
3. 贫苦的 _____ _____

4. 鲜艳的 ____ ____
5. 高超的 ____ ____
6. 精美的 ____ ____

二、选词填空

Fill in the blanks using the words provided.
（此外、比如、结果、吸引、依然、讲究）
1. 高英穿衣服特别 ________，不是名牌的她从来不穿。
2. 我去过中国很多地方，________北京、上海、西安等等。
3. 这个学期我继续学中文，________ 我还修了一门日文课。
4. 十多年不见了，你 ________ 是那么年轻漂亮。
5. 那位歌手的歌声真是 ________ 人，不管门票多贵，场场客满。
6. 李力考试前一天还在玩电脑游戏，________考得很糟糕。

三、用句型造句

Compose sentences using the sentence patterns below.
1. 所 + V + 的
2. 以 …… 为生
3. 为 …… 所 + V
4. 既 …… 又 ……
5. 既然 …… 就 ……
6. V + 不过

四、用本课的成语改写句子

Rewrite each sentence using idioms you have learned in this lesson.
1. 你最近去过大都会博物馆吗？那里展出很多中国古代珍贵的文物呢。
2. 我姐姐住在南方，那儿的树木常绿，花儿常开，没有冬天，美极了。
3. 昨天我们开车回家的时候下大雨、刮大风，什么都看不见了，真够危险的。
4. 你看我急得满头大汗，你却不慌不忙的，一定是心中早就计划好了。

五、选择题

Choose the correct word or phrase to complete each sentence.

1. 国画要求诗、书、画的 ________ 结合。
   a. 完全　　b. 完整
   c. 完美　　d. 完成
2. 画家常常把松、竹、________ 画在一起，叫做"岁寒三友"。
   a. 兰　　　b. 梅
   c. 柏　　　d. 菊
3. 王冕小时候一边给人放 ________，一边念书。
   a. 牛　　　b. 马
   c. 羊　　　d. 鸡
4. 长大后，王冕以 ________ 为生。
   a. 做官　　b. 放牛
   c. 种梅　　d. 卖画
5. 说到画梅，就会想起 ________。
   a. 王羲之　b. 颜真卿
   c. 王冕　　d. 郑板桥
6. ________ 是文房四宝之一，也往往是精美的工艺品。
   a. 笔　　　b. 墨
   c. 纸　　　d. 砚

六、改错

Correct the sentences below.

1. 中国画家喜欢画松树，是因为松树长得好看。
2. 王冕把牛放在草地上，自己到大树下面睡觉去了。
3. 王冕的牛找不到了，结果被他父亲骂了一顿。
4. 王冕自称"兰花屋主"。
5. 人们常用"胸有成竹"来形容郑板桥种了很多竹子。
6. 郑板桥的床头放着一盆兰花。
7. 郑板桥放出黄狗去咬小偷。
8. 中国从唐代起就造纸了。

七、回答问题

Answer the questions below.

1. 国画可分为哪些种类？
2. 为什么很多画家也是诗人和书法家？
3. 举例说明中国画家很重视所画对象的象征意义。
4. 王冕在园子里种了多少梅树？
5. 王冕《墨梅诗》中的前两句说的是什么？
6. 郑板桥以什么著称？
7. 郑板桥怎么知道有小偷来了？
8. 毛笔可分为哪几种？
9. 写书法时，墨要怎样才算磨好了？
10. 什么纸最适合书画？

八、英译中

Translate the passages below into Chinese.

1. Bamboo is widely used in household articles. Bamboo chopsticks are still the most common tableware in China. The *dizi* is made of bamboo. ① People still use paintbrushes made from bamboo today. Bamboo shoots are a popular dish. Tall and graceful with luxuriant foliage, bamboo is an ideal plant for household courtyards and parks. It tolerates the heat of summer and the cold of winter. Also, the bamboo plant is the staple food of the giant panda.

   【生词】① *dizi* 笛子, Chinese flute

2. Zheng Banqiao often had his hair cut at a barbershop run by a man named Wang. Wang had been a barber for ten years, but was too poor to marry. One day Zheng Banqiao gave Wang a big piece of paper, on which was written only the character 一. He said to Wang with a smile, "This is a precious character. Someone will come and pay a great price for it." Sure enough, a few days later a rich man came to Wang's shop and bought the character from him at a high price.

3. It turned out that this rich man wanted to please the county magistrate by presenting him with a board inscribed with characters. So he came to ask Zheng Banqiao to write the two characters 青天 on the board. ① When Zheng Banqiao finished writing, what the rich man saw on the board was 青大. He asked Zheng Banqiao, "Why is the character 天 missing the horizontal stroke at the top?" Zheng Banqiao replied, "Wang has that stroke. Take plenty of

money and go buy it at the barbershop." Having no choice, the rich man went to the barbershop and paid for it. Later, Wang got married with the money he made from selling the character 一, and lived happily ever after.

【生词】① 青天 blue sky, a metaphor for an upright magistrate

九、中译英

Translate the passages below into English.

1. 《清明上河图》①

   中国十大传世名画之一的《清明上河图》是北宋（960-1127）张择端（1085-1145）所画。这幅长卷宽24.8厘米，长528.7厘米，②着重描绘了北宋首都汴梁水陆运输和市面繁忙的景象，具有很高的历史价值和艺术水平。现收藏于北京故宫博物院。在2010年上海世界博览会上，中国馆中展出了电子版的《清明上河图》。通过投影和动画技术创造出来的《清明上河图》，比原作放大了约30倍，实际高6.3米、长130余米。更让人叹为观止的是，《清明上河图》的画面是活动的：流淌的河水、飘动的帆船、往来的市民、客商、骆驼、鸡犬，配以流水潺潺，小贩的吆喝声此起彼伏……画卷的天色还能变化，每四分钟是一个日夜轮回。这幅画以崭新的面貌展示了古代艺术和现代技术的完美结合。

   【生词】①《清明上河图》 "Along the River during the Qingming Festival"

   ② 长卷 long scroll (of painting or calligraphy)

2. 《富春山居图》

   《富春山居图》是元朝（1271-1368）画家黄公望（1269-1354）的杰作，也被誉为中国十大传世名画之一。这幅长卷宽33厘米，长636.9厘米，描绘了浙江富春江的美丽景色，是黄公望为无用师和尚所绘。黄公望78岁高龄时开始作此画，用了六、七年时间，直到他谢世前不久才完成。几百年来，这幅画辗转流失，充满了传奇色彩。明朝（1368-1644）末年传到收藏家吴洪裕手中。吴洪裕极为喜爱此画，甚至在临死前下令将此画焚烧殉葬。吴洪裕的侄子从火中把画抢救出，但此时画已被烧成一大一小两段。前段较小，称《剩山图》，现藏浙江省博物馆；后段较长，称《无用师卷》，现藏台北故宫博物院。经多方协商，浙江的《剩山图》在2011年6月到台湾和《无用师卷》一起展出。时隔三百余年，《富春山居图》终于要以完整面貌重现在世人面前，这是中国绘画史上的一件盛事。

十、故事复述

Retell the following stories:
1. 王冕放牛
2. 郑板桥画《墨竹图》
3. 郑板桥吟诗退贼

十一、课堂辩论

Debate the question posed below.
【题目】中国的国花应该是梅花吗？
【背景】中国还没有决定国花。很多人提议梅花，也有人提议别
的花。
【提示】正方：应该是梅花。梅花和松树、竹子一起是"岁寒三
友"，和兰花、竹子和菊花一起是"四君子"。梅花最早开放，也
很漂亮。反方：应该是一种别的花。你要说明是哪一种，比如
牡丹、菊花、兰花、或荷花，然后说明理由。

十二、作文

Write a short composition of approximately three hundred characters on the
topic below.
【题目】在中国人家中作客【提示】描写你在中国人家中看到
的东西和做的事。什么事情很有趣？跟美国人的家庭有什么不
同？

十三、专题研究

Research the following topics online and report to the class.
1. 介绍一幅名画。
2. 介绍一个有名的画家。

十四、背诵

Recite the following from memory:
1. 王冕《墨梅诗》
2. 郑燮《墨竹诗》

TANG POETRY 唐诗

"A Night Mooring at the Maple Bridge" and "An Occasional Poem upon Returning to My Hometown"
《枫桥夜泊》与《回乡偶书》

唐朝是中国诗歌的黄金时代。直到现在，很多中国家长还教孩子背唐诗。小时候记性好，读了几遍就能记住，而且往往终身不忘。

很多孩子背的第一首诗是李白的《静夜思》："床前明月光，疑是地上霜。举头望明月，低头思故乡。"孩子都背这首诗，可能是因为它很短，用词也很简单，但更主要的是这首诗生动地写出了诗人在旅途中思念家乡的心情。

这里再给大家介绍两首诗。一首是张继的《枫桥夜泊》："月落乌啼霜满天，江枫渔火对愁眠。姑苏城外寒山寺，夜半钟声到客船。"寒山寺在苏州城西，已有一千五百多年的历史。这首诗前两句写了六个景象：月落、乌啼、霜天、江枫、渔火、愁眠。前五个是环境，第六个是主体。霜天说明是深秋，月落说明是下半夜。诗人在船舱中，看着江枫渔火，听着乌啼，无法入睡。在这样的情景中，听到了远处传来的寒山寺的钟声，诗人会有怎样的感觉呢？

另一首是贺知章的《回乡偶书》："少小离家老大回，乡音无改鬓毛衰。儿童相见不相识，笑问客从何处来？"贺知章在八十六岁时辞去官职，回到在浙江的家乡。这首诗用叙事的口气，写得很亲切；但仔细读来，诗中却充满了对比。第一句中的"少小离家"与"老大回"构成一组时间上的对比。实际上，在这两个人生道路的标记中间是五十多年。第二句中的"乡音无改"和"鬓毛衰"又是一组对比，描绘了时间造成的变（年龄）与不变（乡音）。第三句的"相见"与"不相识"对比，以此来说明离家之久。最后一句是儿童的话，非常有趣，但也包含着一组对比，是主客对比：他本是这儿的主人，现在却变成客人了。这四组对比，层层深入，从不同的角度写出他离家半个世纪的伤感，也表达了叶落归根的喜悦。

词汇一 VOCABULARY I

枫	楓	fēng	maple
泊		bó	to moor
偶		ǒu	incidental, accidental, occasional
背		bèi	to recite from memory, to learn by heart
记性	記性	jìxìng	memory
首		shǒu	measure word for poems and songs
往往		wǎngwǎng	常常
终身	終身	zhōngshēn	lifelong
疑		yí	to suspect
霜		shuāng	frost
举	舉	jǔ	to lift
故乡	故鄉	gùxiāng	hometown
生动	生動	shēngdòng	vivid, lively
旅途		lǚtú	journey, trip
思念		sīniàn	to think of, to miss
家乡	家鄉	jiāxiāng	故乡
落		luò	to fall, to drop
乌	烏	wū	crow
啼		tí	(of birds) to caw, to sing
渔火	漁火	yúhuǒ	fishing light
愁		chóu	sad, sorrowful
眠		mián	to sleep
夜半		yèbàn	半夜
船		chuán	boat
景象		jǐngxiàng	scenery, sight
环境	環境	huánjìng	environment
主体	主體	zhǔtǐ	subject, perceiver
船舱	船艙	chuáncāng	cabin

入睡		rùshuì	to fall asleep
情景		qíngjǐng	scene, situation
感觉	感覺	gǎnjué	feeling
少小		shàoxiǎo	at an early age
老大		lǎodà	年老
乡音	鄉音	xiāngyīn	accent of one's native place
改		gǎi	to change
鬓毛	鬢毛	bìnmáo	hair at the temples
衰		cuī	to decline, to thin out
辞（职）	辭（職）	cí	to resign (from a job)
官职	官職	guānzhí	official position
叙事	敍事	xùshì	narrative
口气	口氣	kǒuqi	manner of speaking, tone
亲切	親切	qīnqiè	warm, affectionate
充满	充滿	chōngmǎn	to be full of
对比	對比	duìbǐ	contrast
构成	構成	gòuchéng	to form
标记	標記	biāojì	sign, mark
描绘	描繪	miáohuì	to depict, to describe
年龄	年齡	niánlíng	age
包含		bāohán	to contain, to include
层层	層層	céngcéng	layer upon layer, level by level
深入		shēnrù	to go deep into
角度		jiǎodù	angle, perspective
世纪	世紀	shìjì	century
伤感	傷感	shānggǎn	sorrow
表达	表達	biǎodá	to express
叶落归根	葉落歸根	yèluò guīgēn	falling leaves settle at the roots (a metaphor for a person's eventual return to his native place)
归	歸	guī	to return
喜悦	喜悅	xǐyuè	joy

专名一 PROPER NAMES I

李白		Lǐ Bái	Tang poet (701–762)
张继	張繼	Zhāng Jì	Tang poet (d. 779)
姑苏	姑蘇	Gūsū	ancient name for Suzhou City
寒山寺		Hánshān sì	Cold Mountain Temple in Suzhou
苏州	蘇州	Sūzhōu	city in Jiangsu 江苏 Province
贺知章	賀知章	Hè Zhīzhāng	Tang poet (659–744)

小故事 Ministory
To Push or to Knock 推敲苦吟

　　"推敲"是个常用词，用来比喻写文章或做事时的反复思考。可是为什么叫"推敲"呢？这里有个故事。

　　有一次，唐朝诗人贾岛去长安参加考试。他骑着一头驴子在路上走，脑子里却在想诗句。他想出了两句好诗，在驴背上吟道："鸟宿池边树，僧推月下门。"他觉得很满意，但又打算把"推"字改为"敲"字，一时决定不了，就用手作推、敲的样子。一不小心，驴子冲进一个官员的车队中去，贾岛这才如梦初醒。碰巧，这位官员是大诗人韩愈。听贾岛说了原因之后，韩愈哈哈大笑，对贾岛说："我看还是用'敲'好。晚上去别人家，还是敲门有礼貌呀！而且一个'敲'字，使夜深人静之时，多了一点声音，不是很有趣吗？"贾岛听了连连点头，两人从此成为好朋友。

词汇二 VOCABULARY II

推		tuī	to push
敲		qiāo	to knock
比喻		bǐyù	simile, metaphor, analogy
思考		sīkǎo	to think deeply, to ponder
骑	騎	qí	to ride (a horse, etc.)
头	頭	tóu	measure word for oxen, donkeys, etc.

驴	驢	lú	donkey
背		bèi	back (of the body)
僧		sēng	Buddhist monk
满意	滿意	mǎnyì	pleased, satisfied
一时	一時	yīshí	momentarily
冲	衝	chōng	to charge, to rush
官员	官員	guānyuán	official
车队	車隊	chēduì	convoy, motorcade
梦	夢	mèng	dream
初		chū	first, for the first time, just, presently
醒		xǐng	to wake up, to awaken
碰巧		pèngqiǎo	coincidentally
礼貌	禮貌	lǐmào	courtesy, manners
连连	連連	liánlián	again and again

专名二 PROPER NAMES II

贾岛	賈島	Jiǎ Dǎo	Tang poet (779-843)
长安	長安	Cháng'ān	Tang capital, present-day Xi'an 西安
韩愈	韓愈	Hán Yù	Tang poet (768-825)

小知识 Knowledge

The Tolling Bell at Hanshan Temple 寒山钟声

　　自从张继写了《枫桥夜泊》这首诗以后，寒山寺的钟声变得非常有名。苏州市从1979年开始举办"寒山寺除夕夜听钟声"的活动，已成为一个传统，每年有几千名中外人士参加。寒山寺的钟声从除夕夜的二十三点四十二分十秒开始敲响，十秒一次，到新年O点O秒为止，共一百O八响。这一百O八响有两层除旧迎新的意思。一是农历有十二个月、二十四个节气、七十二个候，加起来正好一百O八。听过钟声，一年算是过去了。二是佛教认为人生有很多烦恼，一共一百O八个，听了钟声，可以层层解脱，新的一年中能平平安安。有这么好的事，你也想去寒山寺听钟声吗？

词汇三 VOCABULARY III

举办	舉辦	jǔbàn	to hold, to sponsor (an event, etc.)
除夕		chúxī	New Year's Eve
人士		rénshì	people
秒		miǎo	second (a unit of time)
为止	為止	wéizhǐ	until, up to
止		zhǐ	stop, end
除旧迎新	除舊迎新	chújiù yíngxīn	to ring out the old and ring in the new
除		chú	to eliminate
农历	農曆	nónglì	Chinese lunar calendar
节气	節氣	jiéqì	one of the twenty-four seasonal division points in the Chinese lunar calendar
候		hòu	each of the five days in the Chinese lunar calendar
佛教		fójiào	Buddhism
烦恼	煩惱	fánnǎo	vexation, worry
解脱	解脫	jiětuō	to extricate
平安		píng'ān	safe and sound

语言点 Language Points

一、词语 WORDS

1. 往往 often

【课文】小时候记性好，读了几遍就能记住，而且往往终身不忘。

【例句】电影里干坏事的人往往没有好结果，生活中呢？

People who do bad things in movies often do not meet with good ends. What about in life?

2. 对比 contrast

【课文】这首诗用叙事的口气，写得很亲切；但仔细读来，诗中却充满了对比。

【例句】这件衬衫大红大绿的，颜色对比太大，你穿不好看。

This shirt has distinct reds and greens, and too sharp a color contrast; you don't look good wearing it.

3. 描绘 to depict, to describe

【课文】第二句中的"乡音无改"和"鬓毛衰"又是一组对比，描绘了时间造成的变（年龄）与不变（乡音）。

【例句】在这篇文章里，他用了很多描绘春天的形容词和比喻句，生动而且形象。

He used many adjectives and metaphors to describe spring in this article; it is lively and vivid.

4. 包含 to contain, to include

【课文】最后一句是儿童的话，非常有趣，但也包含着一组对比。

【例句】我的暑假计划包含的内容可多了：先去中国学习，回来修一门网上的课，然后去打工，此外还要打网球，实在太忙了。

My summer plans include so many things: first, I will go to China to study; after I come back, I will take a course online; then I will get a job; besides that, I will play tennis. I will be really busy.

5. 碰巧 coincidentally

【课文】碰巧，这位官员是大诗人韩愈。

【例句】一到我们吃饭的时候，他就会出现，然后说是碰巧路过。

Whenever we had a meal, he would appear, saying that he'd happened to pass by.

6. 却 but, yet

【课文】这首诗用叙事的口气，写得很亲切；但仔细读来，诗中却充满了对比。

【例句】他对他的女朋友真是百依百顺，可他的女朋友对他却总是爱理不理的样子。

He's at his girlfriend's beck and call, but his girlfriend is always indifferent to him.

7. 算是 to be counted as, to be considered

【课文】听过钟声，一年算是过去了。

【例句】在酒吧里做中文功课——我不知道你这算是用功呢，还是不用功？

You do your Chinese homework at the bar—I am not sure whether this is considered diligence.

二、句型 SENTENCE PATTERNS

1. 从……角度 from . . . angle, perspective

【课文】第三句的"相见"与"不相识"对比，从小辈都不认识他的角度来说明离家之久。

【例句】从目前经济的角度考虑，现在还不是买房子的最好时机。

From a current economic perspective, this is not the best time to buy a house.

2. 本是……现在却 was originally . . . but now

【课文】他本是这儿的主人，现在却变成客人了。

【例句】这个地方本是乡下，现在却发展成热闹的城市了。

This place was originally a village, but now it has developed into a bustling city.

3. 觉得……但又 to feel . . . but also

【课文】他觉得很满意，但又打算把"推"字改为"敲"字，一时决定不了。

【例句】他心里一直觉得很对不起那个女孩，但又不知道怎么跟她说对不起。

He always feels he is unfair to that girl, but he does not know how to say sorry to her.

4. 自从……以后 since, after

【课文】自从张继写了《枫桥夜泊》这首诗以后，寒山寺的钟声变得非常有名。

【例句】自从他开始学中文以后，他对中国的文化和历史越来越感兴趣了。

Since he started learning Chinese, his interest in Chinese culture and history has grown stronger and stronger.

三、成语 IDIOMS

1. 叶落归根 falling leaves settle at the roots (a metaphor for a person's eventual return to his native place)

【课文】这四组对比从不同的角度写出他离家半个世纪的伤感，也表达了叶落归根的喜悦。

【例句】王先生七十岁的时候就说要叶落归根，现在八十岁了，还没回去。

Mr. Wang said when he was seventy that he would return to his homeland. However, he is now eighty but has not gone back yet.

2. 如梦初醒 as if one were awakening from a dream, to wake up to

【课文】一不小心，驴子冲进一个官员的车队中去，贾岛这才如梦初醒。

【例句】林达成毕业后什么工作都找不到，这才如梦初醒：他选错了专业。

Lin Dacheng could not find a job after graduation, and only then did he wake up: he'd chosen the wrong major.

3. 夜深人静 quiet, deep night

【课文】一个"敲"字，使夜深人静之时，多了一点声音，不是很有趣吗？

【例句】那位作家常常是白天睡大觉，到晚上夜深人静时才写文章。

That writer often sleeps through the day; he does not write until everything quiets down deep in the night.

4. 除旧迎新 to ring out the old and ring in the new

【课文】这一百〇八响有两层除旧迎新的意思。

【例句】中国人喜欢在除夕打扫房子，这也是一种除旧迎新的风俗。

Chinese people like to clean house on New Year's Eve; this is also a custom of leaving behind the old and welcoming the new.

练习 Exercises

一、填名词

Fill in the blanks with appropriate nouns to form adjective-noun phrases.

1. 生动的 ＿＿＿ ＿＿＿
2. 亲切的 ＿＿＿ ＿＿＿
3. 仔细的 ＿＿＿ ＿＿＿
4. 伤感的 ＿＿＿ ＿＿＿
5. 喜悦的 ＿＿＿ ＿＿＿
6. 有趣的 ＿＿＿ ＿＿＿

二、选词填空

Fill in the blanks using the words provided.

（往往、对比、包含、描绘、碰巧、却、算是）

1. 这位画家的特点是喜欢运用强烈的色彩 ＿＿＿ ＿＿＿。
2. 我这次考试考得好 ＿＿＿ ＿＿＿ 运气好，因为考试的题目我都猜到了。
3. 早上出门天气那么晴朗，下午 ＿＿＿ 突然下起雨来了，真是天有不测风云啊。
4. 要写好一篇文章，很重要的一条是对人和事物进行具体的 ＿＿＿ ＿＿＿。
5. 昨天我去商店买东西，＿＿＿ ＿＿＿ 遇到了一位好久不见的小学同学。
6. 这个公司的计划 ＿＿＿ ＿＿＿ 的内容非常丰富，看来我们今天的会议要开到半夜了。
7. 这个考试虽然不难，但你们也要仔细地做，简单的题目 ＿＿＿ ＿＿＿ 容易做错。

三、用句型造句

Compose sentences using the sentence patterns below.

1. 从……角度
2. 本是……现在却

3. 觉得……但又
4. 自从……以后

四、用本课的成语改写句子

Rewrite each sentence using idioms you have learned in this lesson.

1. 李龙今天上课一直在睡觉，老师叫他回答问题时，他才慢慢睁开眼睛，全班都笑了。
2. 鹿常常在半夜里人们睡觉的时候出来吃我花园里的花儿，真拿它们没办法。
3. 我的父母年轻时从中国来美国，他们现在想退休后回中国去。
4. 小明，今天是新年，你要穿件新衣服，这也是庆祝新年啊。

五、选择题

Choose the correct word or phrase to complete each sentence.

1. ________ 是中国诗歌的黄金时代。
    a. 汉朝　　b. 唐朝
    c. 宋朝　　d. 明朝
2. 很多孩子背的第一首诗是 ________ 的《静夜思》。
    a. 王冕　　b. 张继
    c. 郑燮　　d. 李白
3. 《静夜思》________ 地写出了诗人在旅途中思念家乡的感情。
    a. 生动　　b. 亲切
    c. 仔细　　d. 有趣
4. 寒山寺在 ________ 城西。
    a. 上海　　b. 北京
    c. 西安　　d. 苏州
5. 《枫桥夜泊》的前两句写了六个 ________。
    a. 现象　　b. 对象
    c. 景象　　d. 印象
6. 霜天说明是 ________。
    a. 早春　　b. 初夏
    c. 深秋　　d. 寒冬

7. 听到远处传来的寒山寺的钟声，诗人会有怎样的 _________ 呢？
   a. 感情　　　b. 感想
   c. 感觉　　　d. 感谢

8. 贺知章的《回乡偶书》中充满了_________。
   a. 对比　　　b. 对象
   c. 对面　　　d. 对子

9. 贾岛骑着一 _________ 驴子在路上走。
   a. 匹　　　　b. 头
   c. 条　　　　d. 口

10. 每年有几千名中外 _________ 参加。
   a. 人民　　　b. 人员
   c. 人们　　　d. 人士

六、改错

Correct the sentences below.

1. 很多孩子背的第一首诗是张继的《枫桥夜泊》。
2. 寒山寺已有五百多年的历史。
3. 月落说明是上半夜。
4. 诗人在船舱中，看着江枫渔火，听着鸟啼，无法入睡。
5. 实际上，在这两个人生道路的标记中间是八十六年。
6. 有一次，唐朝诗人贾岛去北京参加考试。
7. 如梦初醒是说早上起床的意思。
8. 苏州市从1979年开始举办"寒山寺圣诞夜听钟声"的活动。

七、回答问题

Answer the questions below.

1. 李白的《静夜思》好在哪里？
2. 张继的《枫桥夜泊》的前两句写了哪六个景象？
3. 贺知章的《回乡偶书》用的是什么口气？
4. 贺知章离家五十多年，什么变了？什么没变？
5. 《回乡偶书》写出了诗人什么样的感情？
6. 贾岛的驴子怎么会冲进韩愈的车队中去？
7. 为什么韩愈说是"敲"字好？
8. 为什么寒山寺的钟声在除夕夜要敲一百○八响？

八、英译中

Translate the passages below into Chinese.

1. In the Tang dynasty (618–906), China became the hub of the Eastern world, and all roads from Asia led to Chang'an, its most magnificent metropolis. This was an era of brilliant intellectual and literary activities unsurpassed by any other period in Chinese history. The splendor and the subsequent decline of the Tang period are reflected in its poetry. Tang China, like Elizabethan England, was virtually a nation of singing birds. Even through the lapse of more than a millennium, a large body of Tang poetry, consisting of approximately 50,000 poems by some 2,300 poets, has been preserved to this day.

2. The writing of poetry, which has attracted the Chinese people since ancient times, became especially popular during the Tang dynasty. Poets were honored by the public and, in a number of instances, received the patronage of the court. The majority of Tang poets were officials who had passed the civil service examinations but whose claim to fame was based not so much on their administrative ability as on their poetic achievements. There were also numerous poets among the ranks of emperors and empresses, generals and courtiers, Daoist hermits and Buddhist monks, and court ladies and singing girls, who together contributed to the greatness of Tang poetry.

九、中译英

Translate the poems below into English.

1. 孟浩然 《春晓》
   春眠不觉晓，处处闻啼鸟。夜来风雨声，花落知多少？
2. 李绅 《悯农》
   锄禾日当午，汗滴禾下土。谁知盘中餐，粒粒皆辛苦。
3. 王之涣 《登鹳雀楼》
   白日依山尽，黄河入海流。欲穷千里目，更上一层楼。

十、故事复述

Retell the following story:

1. 推敲苦吟

十一、课堂辩论

Debate the question posed below.

【题目】背唐诗有用吗？

【提示】正方：小时候记性好，背的时候即使不全懂，慢慢会加深理解。小时候背的诗，终身不忘，终身有用。反方：死记硬背是旧法子。学习主要是要理解。唐朝离我们太远了，我听了寒山寺的钟声也不会有感觉。

十二、作文

Write a short composition of approximately three hundred characters on the topic below.

【题目】旅行途中

【提示】结合旅行途中看到的景物，写出自己当时的思想和感情。

十三、专题研究

Research the following topics online and report to the class.

1. 介绍一首唐诗。
2. 介绍一个唐代的诗人。

十四、背诵

Recite the following from memory:

1. 李白《静夜思》
2. 张继《枫桥夜泊》
3. 贺知章《回乡偶书》

CHINESE INSTRUMENTAL MUSIC 民乐

"The High Mountain and Flowing Water" and "Ambush from All Sides"
《高山流水》与《十面埋伏》

中国的传统音乐也叫民族音乐，简称民乐。民乐有很多独特的乐器和经典曲目。

琴，也叫古琴，是中国最古老的弹拨乐器，据说有五千多年的历史。琴曲《高山流水》叙述了一个动人的故事。

春秋时代，有个著名的琴师叫伯牙。一天，伯牙在山上弹琴，有个名叫钟子期的樵夫在边上听了很久。子期告诉伯牙，他听出乐曲表现了高高的泰山和奔流的黄河。伯牙激动地说："我弹的是古曲《高山流水》。你真是我的知音啊！"

两人约定，明年这个时候还在这儿相会。第二年，伯牙到了山上，却不见子期。原来，子期已经去世了。伯牙来到子期的坟墓前，悲伤地弹起了《高山流水》。弹完后，他长叹一声，把心爱的琴在青石上摔碎了。他说："我的知音已不在人世了，这琴还能弹给谁听呢？"后来，人们在他们相遇的地方，造了一座琴台。直至今天，人们还用"知音"来形容互相了解的好朋友。

跟优雅的《高山流水》不同，琵琶曲《十面埋伏》的旋律是激动人心的。

《十面埋伏》用音乐表现了历史上有名的楚汉大战。秦朝末年，各地起义，最强的两支军队是刘邦领导的汉军和项羽领导的楚军。公元前202年，刘邦以三十万兵力，包围并消灭了项羽的十万军队。战后，刘邦建立了汉朝。

这首乐曲充分运用了琵琶高超的技巧，再现惊心动魄的战争场面，使人仿佛能听到战鼓声、军号声、叫喊声、马蹄声和兵器打击声。难怪有人说，一个琵琶的独奏，比得上一支交响乐队。

词汇一 VOCABULARY I

十面埋伏		shímiàn máifú	ambush from all sides
民族		mínzú	nationality, ethnic group
独特	獨特	dútè	unique, distinctive
乐器	樂器	yuèqì	musical instrument
经典	經典	jīngdiǎn	classical
曲目		qǔmù	repertoire
琴		qín	*qin*, a seven-stringed plucked instrument similar in some ways to the zither
弹拨	彈撥	tánbō	to pluck
据说	據說	jùshuō	it is said, reportedly
叙述	敘述	xùshù	to narrate, to recount
樵夫	樵夫	qiáofū	woodcutter
奔流		bēnliú	to rush on in a torrent
坟墓	墳墓	fénmù	grave, tomb
悲伤	悲傷	bēishāng	sad, mournful
摔		shuāi	to hurl, to fling
碎		suì	broken
相遇		xiāngyù	to meet, to come across
台	臺	tái	terrace, stage
直至		zhízhì	until, up to
优雅	優雅	yōuyǎ	elegant, graceful
琵琶		pípá	*pipa*, a plucked stringed instrument with a fretted fingerboard
旋律		xuánlǜ	melody
大战	大戰	dàzhàn	great war, great battle
末年		mònián	last years (of a dynasty or reign)
起义	起義	qǐyì	uprising, insurrection
领导	領導	lǐngdǎo	to lead
公元前		gōngyuánqián	BCE (before the Common Era)
以		yǐ	用
兵力		bīnglì	armed forces
消灭	消滅	xiāomiè	to annihilate

充分		chōngfèn	fully
运用	運用	yùnyòng	to utilize, to apply
技巧		jìqiǎo	skill, technique
惊心动魄	驚心動魄	jīngxīn dòngpò	stirring, fiercely intense
战争	戰爭	zhànzhēng	war
场面	場面	chǎngmiàn	scene
仿佛	仿佛	fǎngfú	好像, as if
鼓		gǔ	drum
军号	軍號	jūnhào	bugle
叫喊		jiàohǎn	to shout, to yell
马蹄	馬蹄	mǎtí	horse's hoof
兵器	兵器	bīngqì	weapon
打击	打擊	dǎjī	to strike
独奏	獨奏	dúzòu	(in instrumental music) solo
比得上		bǐdéshàng	to be as good as
交响乐队	交響樂隊	jiāoxiǎng yuèduì	symphony orchestra

专名一　PROPER NAMES I

春秋		Chūnqiū	Spring and Autumn period (722–481 BCE)
伯牙		Bóyá	a legendary *qin* master
钟子期	鍾子期	Zhōng Zǐqī	personal name
泰山		Tàishān	Mount Tai, a mountain of historical and cultural significance, located in present-day Shandong 山东 Province
楚		Chǔ	name of Xiang Yu's army
刘邦	劉邦	Liú Bāng	Emperor Gaozu (r. 202–195 BCE), founder of the Han dynasty
项羽	項羽	Xiàng Yǔ	Chu general (232–202 BCE)

小故事 Ministory

Butterflies among the Flowers 花间彩蝶

你听过小提琴协奏曲《梁祝》吗？你知道这个爱情故事吗？

古时候，有个美丽、好学的姑娘叫祝英台。她一心想去杭州读书。那时候女孩子不能上学，她就扮成男人上了路。

在学校里，英台跟同学梁山伯成为好朋友。在三年同学期间，英台爱上了山伯，但山伯却始终不知她是个女子。

祝英台的父亲想念女儿，催她回家。梁山伯依依不舍地送了她十八里路。分别时，英台对山伯说，她家中有一个妹妹，要山伯去祝家求婚。过了一段时间，等山伯到祝家时，才知道英台是个姑娘。但是祝父已答应把英台嫁给一个大官的儿子。山伯知道后很伤心，不久就生病去世了。

英台被迫出嫁前，来到梁山伯墓前。英台的悲伤感动了天地，在狂风暴雨中，山伯的坟墓裂开，英台跳了进去。过了一会儿，风雨停了，彩虹高挂在天上，梁祝化成蝴蝶，在百花中飞舞。

这个故事后来改编成越剧，结束时演员齐声唱道："彩虹万里百花开，花间彩蝶成双对。千年万代分不开，梁山伯与祝英台。"

词汇二 VOCABULARY II

彩		cǎi	color, colorful
（蝴）蝶		(hú)dié	butterfly
小提琴		xiǎotíqín	violin
协奏曲	協奏曲	xiézòuqǔ	concerto
爱情	愛情	àiqíng	love
好学	好學	hàoxué	to be fond of learning
一心		yīxīn	wholeheartedly, earnestly

扮		bàn	to disguise
想念		xiǎngniàn	to long to see again, to miss
催		cuī	to push, to press, to hurry
依依不舍		yīyī bùshě	to be reluctant to part with
依		yī	to depend on, to rely on
舍（得）		shěde	to be ready to part with or give up
分别		fēnbié	to part
求婚		qiúhūn	to propose marriage
答应	答應	dāying	to agree, to promise
嫁	嫁	jià	(of a woman) to marry
伤心	傷心	shāngxīn	sad, brokenhearted
被迫	被迫	bèipò	to be compelled
裂		liè	to split, to crack
停		tíng	to stop, to cease, to halt
虹		hóng	rainbow
化		huà	to transform
改编	改編	gǎibiān	to adapt
齐声	齊聲	qíshēng	to be in chorus, in unison

专名二 PROPER NAMES II

祝英台	Zhù Yīngtái	personal name
杭州	Hángzhōu	city in Zhejiang Province
梁山伯	Liáng Shānbó	personal name

小知识 Knowledge
Erhu and *suona* 二胡唢呐

本课课文中讲到古琴和琵琶两种民族乐器，这里再介绍两种。

二胡是民乐中主要的弓弦乐器之一，它的作用有点儿像西方乐队中的小提琴。因为是用两根弦拉奏，所以叫二胡。著名的二胡独奏曲有《二泉映月》等。

唢呐又名喇叭，是个吹奏乐器，广泛应用于各种民间仪式。

以前送嫁妆、跟花轿、办喜酒、闹洞房、回娘家等喜庆活动，都少不了唢呐。唢呐名曲《百鸟朝凤》以欢快的旋律与百鸟的叫声，表现了生气勃勃的大自然。

词汇三 VOCABULARY III

二胡		èrhú	*erhu*, a two-stringed Chinese fiddle
弓		gōng	bow
弦		xián	string (on an instrument)
作用		zuòyòng	role, function
拉		lā	to play a certain musical instrument, such as *erhu* or violin
泉		quán	spring (water)
唢呐		suǒnà	*suona*, a woodwind horn
喇叭		lǎbā	trumpet, horn
吹奏		chuīzòu	to play (wind instruments)
广泛	廣泛	guǎngfàn	wide, broad
应用	應用	yīngyòng	to use, to apply
于		yú	在
民间	民間	mínjiān	customary, conventional, folk
仪式	儀式	yíshì	ceremony, rite
嫁妆	嫁妝	jiàzhuāng	dowry
花轿	花轎	huājiào	bridal sedan chair, palanquin
喜酒		xǐjiǔ	wedding banquet
闹	鬧	nào	noisy
洞房		dòngfáng	nuptial chamber
娘家		niángjiā	home of a married woman's parents
喜庆	喜慶	xǐqìng	jubilant and festive
朝		cháo	to face, to pay respect to, to worship
凤		fèng	phoenix
欢快	歡快	huānkuài	merry and lively
生气勃勃	生氣勃勃	shēngqì bóbó	vigorous

语言点 Language Points

一、词语 WORDS

1. 据说 it is said

   【课文】琴，也叫古琴，是中国最古老的弹拨乐器，据说有五千多年的历史。

   【例句】你最近跟小英打过电话吗？据说她已经结婚了。

   Have you called Xiaoying recently? It is said that she got married.

2. 难怪 no wonder

   【课文】难怪有人说，一个琵琶的独奏，比得上一个交响乐队。

   【例句】他是家里的独生子，难怪全家人都把他当成"小皇帝"。

   He is the only son at home; no wonder the whole family treated him like a "little emperor."

3. 比得上 to be as good as

   【课文】难怪有人说，一个琵琶的独奏，比得上一个交响乐队。

   【例句】无论店里的东西多好吃，还是比不上妈妈亲手包的饺子。

   No matter how delicious the food in the restaurant is, it still cannot compare to the dumplings mom makes.

4. 始终 from beginning to end

   【课文】山伯却始终不知她是个女子。

   【例句】虽然我听这个教授讲课就要打瞌睡，但我始终坚信美国的大学教育是世界一流的。

   Although I always doze off during this professor's lectures, I believe from beginning to end that higher education in the United States is first rate.

5. 被迫 to be compelled

   【课文】英台被迫出嫁前，来到梁山伯墓前。

   【例句】由于家境穷困，她被迫退学，小小年纪就得去打工。

   Because of her poor family situation, she was forced to quit school and go to work at an early age.

6. 有点儿 a little

【课文】二胡的作用有点儿像西方乐队中的小提琴。

【例句】这碗汤的味道有点儿怪，大概你把糖当成盐了吧？

This soup tastes a little strange. Perhaps you took salt to be sugar?

7. 少不了 cannot do without

【课文】以前送嫁妆、跟花轿、办喜酒、闹洞房，回娘家等喜庆活动，都少不了唢呐手。

【例句】七月四号是美国的国庆日，全国各地都会举行各种庆祝活动，放烟花是绝对少不了的。

The Fourth of July is a national holiday in the United States. There will be celebrations all over the country and it would not do to have no fireworks.

二、句型 SENTENCE PATTERNS

1. 直至……还 up to . . . still

【课文】直至今天，人们还用"知音"来形容朋友之间的了解和友谊。

【例句】因为唐朝时中国的经济文化很发达，所以直至今天，很多华侨还自称"唐人"。

Because China's economy and culture were highly developed in the Tang dynasty, even now many overseas Chinese still call themselves "Tang People."

2. 跟……不同 different from

【课文】跟优雅的《高山流水》不同，琵琶曲《十面埋伏》的旋律是激动人心的。

【例句】我跟你不同，你太骄傲了，而谦虚是我的美德。

I am different from you: you are too arrogant, but modesty is my virtue.

3. 以（用）……V to do something with

【课文】刘邦以三十万兵力，包围并消灭了项羽的十万军队。

【例句】妈妈一说今天出去吃饭，小明就以最快的速度，把功课全做好了。

As soon as mom said that we would be eating out today, Xiaoming finished all his homework extremely quickly.

4. 在 …… 期间 during (a particular period)

【课文】在三年同学期间，英台爱上了山伯。

【例句】在大学四年期间，我认识了很多人，但真正的好朋友却只有一个，那就是你。

I became acquainted with many people during my four years of college, but I had only one true friend, and that is you.

5. 等（到）…… 才 to do something only after

【课文】等山伯到祝家时，才知道英台是个姑娘。

【例句】人常常要等到失去什么，才会明白它的价值。

One often comes to know the value of something only after it has been lost.

三、 成语 IDIOMS

1. 激动人心 exciting, stirring

【课文】跟优雅的《高山流水》不同，琵琶曲《十面埋伏》的旋律是激动人心的。

【例句】今天的音乐会真是激动人心，很多人都跟着歌唱家唱了起来。

Today's concert was very exciting; many people started to sing along with the singer.

2. 惊心动魄 stirring, fiercely intense

【课文】这首乐曲充分运用了琵琶高超的技巧，再现惊心动魄的战争场面。

【例句】这场篮球赛真是惊心动魄，两个队的比分始终只差一、两分。

This basketball game was really stirring; the teams were only one or two points apart from beginning to end.

3. 依依不舍 to be reluctant to part with

【课文】梁山伯依依不舍地送她送了她十八里路。

【例句】每次跟男朋友分手的时候，她总是依依不舍，好像还有很多话没说完。

Each time, she was always reluctant to part with her boyfriend; it was as if she still had much to say.

4. 生气勃勃 vigorous

【课文】唢呐名曲《百鸟朝凤》以热情欢快的旋律与百鸟的叫声，表现了生气勃勃的大自然。

【例句】春天来了，小草开始绿了，树上长出了嫩叶，花儿张开了笑脸，小鸟唱起歌来……到处是一派生气勃勃的景象。

Spring has arrived, the grass has started to turn green, tender leaves are growing on the trees, flowers open their smiling faces, little birds are starting to sing … everywhere is full of life.

练习 Exercises

一、填名词

Fill in the blanks with appropriate nouns to form adjective-noun phrases.

1. 独特的 ＿＿＿ ＿＿＿
2. 著名的 ＿＿＿ ＿＿＿
3. 优雅的 ＿＿＿ ＿＿＿
4. 激动的 ＿＿＿ ＿＿＿
5. 高超的 ＿＿＿ ＿＿＿
6. 热情的 ＿＿＿ ＿＿＿
7. 欢快的 ＿＿＿ ＿＿＿

二、选词填空

Fill in the blanks using the words provided.

（据说、难怪、比得上、始终、被迫、有点儿、少不了）

1. 我把"妈麻马骂"念了几十遍，可是我 ＿＿＿＿＿＿＿ 分不清四声，你还有什么好办法？
2. 小玲跳舞跳得好极了，每次学生活动 ＿＿＿＿＿＿＿ 她的节目。
3. 他昨天晚上一夜没睡，＿＿＿＿＿＿＿ 今天上课时睡着了。
4. 为了挣钱养活家人，李先生 ＿＿＿＿＿＿＿ 远离家乡，去很远的大城市打工。
5. 我们大学的辩论队年年得全国冠军，没有哪个学校 ＿＿＿＿＿＿＿。

6. 看你的脸，我就知道你今天 _________ 不高兴。有什么心事？快
　　告诉我吧。

7. 这个新药 _________ 非常好，你要试一试吗？

三、用句型造句

Compose sentences using the sentence patterns below.

1. 直至……还
2. 跟……不同
3. 以（用）……V
4. 在……期间
5. 等（到）……才

四、用本课的成语改写句子

Rewrite each sentence using idioms you have learned in this lesson.

1. 儿童合唱团来表演了，养老院里立刻就显得非常有生气。
2. 今天机场里人特别多，到处是送行的场面。
3. 这位市长的演说常常能使人觉得很感动，可是他讲完了就什么
　　事儿也不干。
4. 这个电影里的打斗场面真是非常紧张，我看得手心里都出汗
　　了。

五、选择题

Choose the correct word or phrase to complete each sentence.

1. 伯牙激动地说："我弹的是古曲《 _________ 》。你真是我的知
　　音啊！"
　　　　a. 十面埋伏　　　b. 二泉映月
　　　　c. 百鸟朝凤　　　d. 高山流水

2. 这首乐曲充分运用了琵琶 _________ 的技巧，再现惊心动魄的战
　　争场面。
　　　　a. 高超　　　　　b. 优雅
　　　　c. 热情　　　　　d. 激动

3. _________ 有人说，一个琵琶的独奏，比得上一个交响乐队。
    a. 仿佛   b. 始终
    c. 难怪   d. 广泛

4. 你听过 _________ 协奏曲《梁祝》吗？
    a. 琵琶   b. 古琴
    c. 小提琴   d. 大提琴

5. 祝英台一心想去 _________ 读书。
    a. 杭州   b. 苏州
    c. 常州   d. 广州

6. 唢呐又名喇叭，是个 _________ 乐器。
    a. 弹拨   b. 吹奏
    c. 弓弦   d. 打击

六、改错

Correct the sentences below.

1. 琵琶是中国最古老的弹拨乐器。

2. 战国时代，有个著名的琴师叫伯牙。

3. 一天，伯牙在山上弹琴，有个名叫钟子期的渔夫在边上听了很久。

4. 子期告诉伯牙，他听出乐曲表现了高高的泰山和奔流的长江。

5. 伯牙来到琴台，悲伤地弹起了《二泉映月》。

6. 周朝末年，各地起义，最强的两支军队是刘邦领导的汉军和项羽领导的楚军。

7. 公元前202年，刘邦以二十万兵力，包围并消灭了项羽的十万军队。

8. 战后，刘邦建立了唐朝。

9. 在三年同学期间，山伯爱上了英台。

10. 山伯在读书时，就知道英台是个姑娘。

11. 祝父答应把英台嫁给一个大官。

12. 英台被迫出嫁前，来到梁山伯家里。

13. 过了一会儿，风雨停了，太阳高挂在天上。

七、 回答问题

Answer the questions below.

1. 中国的传统音乐简称什么？
2. 中国最古老的弹拨乐器是什么？
3. 古琴有多少年的历史了？
4. 为什么伯牙说钟子期是他的知音？
5. 为什么伯牙把他心爱的琴在青石上摔碎了？
6. 人们在伯牙和子期相遇的地方造了什么？
7. 人们用"知音"来形容什么？
8. 《十面埋伏》表现了什么故事？
9. 在《十面埋伏》中能听到哪些声音？
10. 为什么祝英台要女扮男装？
11. 梁山伯与祝英台化成什么？

八、 英译中

Translate the passages below into Chinese.

1. "Moon Reflecting on the Second Fountain" 二泉映月

   "Moon Reflecting on the Second Fountain" is a beautiful and moving piece of *erhu* music, composed by a talented folk musician named Hua Yanjun 华彦钧 (1893–1950) in the city of Wuxi 无锡, in Jiangsu Province. Poor and blind, he was known as Blind A Bing 瞎子阿炳. The "Second Fountain" refers to the Huishan 惠山 Fountain in Wuxi, which was praised as the "Second Fountain under Heaven" 天下第二泉. A Bing often played the *erhu* next to the Second Fountain, but he barely earned enough to feed himself. This song describes scenes of the beautiful Second Spring at night, accompanied by a sorrowful mood. Having heard of his music, professors of the prestigious Central Conservatory in Beijing interviewed him and recorded his performance of "Moon Reflecting on the Second Fountain" in 1950. A Bing promised that he would record more than two hundred of his *erhu* pieces. Sadly, he passed away due to illness in December that year. "Moon Reflecting on the Second Fountain" quickly became a classic *erhu* piece and was adapted for a violin solo and a string quartet.

2. "Hundred Birds Worshiping the Phoenix" 百鸟朝凤

The best-known piece for *suona* is "Hundred Birds Worshiping the Phoenix." With the accompaniment of an orchestra, the *suona* plays a vigorous, piping tune in imitation of the chirping of birds in flight. The closeness of the mimicry expresses a love for nature, the intense scrutiny of ordinary life by folk artists, as well as their virtuosity. This song also has rich cultural connotations. In ancient China, the phoenix was first used to represent emperors, then to symbolize empresses when paired with the dragon, which became the symbol of emperors. Thus, this metaphor of "Hundred Birds Worshiping the Phoenix" can also be used to express people's wishes for a time of peace and prosperity. The beautiful and auspicious melodies of this piece were adapted for solo piano in 1973—this piece by the same name quickly became a favorite of many pianists.

九、中译英

Translate the passages below into English.

1. 浙江省的宁波市是梁祝故事的发源地，梁山伯在那儿做过官。宁波有一座以梁祝爱情故事为主题的梁祝公园。根据故事情节，兴建了很多景点，如梁祝读书的学校、梁山伯送祝英台回家的道路、祝英台的家及梁山伯的墓地等。

2. 越剧《梁山伯与祝英台》被称为"中国的《罗密欧与朱丽叶》"。①两个戏有很多相象的地方。两对年轻人都追求自由的爱情，都受到家长的激烈反对。结局都是在墓地，都是女的追随男的死去。很多观众看这两个戏的时候都哭得很伤心。

　　【生词】①《罗密欧与朱丽叶》：*Romeo and Juliet*

3. 但是这两个戏也有很多不同的地方。梁山伯与祝英台是经过三年同学，慢慢相爱的，而罗密欧与朱丽叶是在一场舞会中一见钟情。梁山伯与祝英台最后化成蝴蝶，得到团圆，非常富有诗意。所以有的观众也就破涕为笑了。

十、故事复述

Retell the following stories:

1. 高山流水
2. 十面埋伏
3. 花间彩蝶

十一、课堂辩论

Debate the question posed below.

【题目】祝英台应该跳进梁山伯的坟墓吗？

【提示】正方：应该。失去了她爱的人，没有了爱情，她活着也没有意思了。她的死表示了她对爱情的看法。反方：不应该。人生有很多选择。而且，她爸爸给她找的大官的儿子也不一定不好。

十二、作文

Write a short composition of approximately three hundred characters on the topic below.

【题目】听《梁祝》【提示】你可先在英文或中文的网站上读《梁祝》的故事，然后在YouTube上欣赏《梁祝》小提琴协奏曲的演奏。你听到哪些高兴的和悲伤的音乐段落？反映了哪些故事情节？你是不是受到了感动？

十三、专题研究

Research the following topics online and report to the class.

1. 介绍一个中国民乐乐器。
2. 介绍一个中国民乐乐曲。

BEIJING OPERA 京剧

The White Snake and *The Empty City Stratagem*
《白蛇传》与《空城计》

京剧是一门综合的艺术，运用了戏剧、歌唱、器乐、舞蹈、武术、化妆等许多艺术手段。京剧的化妆很有特色。性格或相貌上有些特异的男角色，化妆用脸谱，叫"花脸"。红色的脸谱表示忠诚，黑色的脸谱表示勇猛，黄色表示凶狠，蓝色或绿色表示暴躁，白色表示奸诈。

京剧的很多剧目改编自历史故事或民间传说。《白蛇传》就是一个著名的民间传说。故事的开始发生在宋朝时的杭州。一个名叫许仙的年轻人在美丽的西湖上遇见了白蛇变成的白娘子和青蛇变成的小青。许仙和白娘子产生了爱情，并结成夫妇。婚后，他们搬到镇江居住，开了一家药店，生活非常幸福。可是，镇江金山寺的和尚法海想方设法要拆散许仙和白娘子。他用法术将白娘子收入他的钵内，压在西湖边的雷峰塔下。后来，小青打败法海，推倒雷峰塔，救出白娘子。

京剧表演的更多的是历史故事。《空城计》讲的是历史小说《三国演义》中的诸葛亮的故事。汉朝末年，中国分成魏、蜀、吴三国。蜀国的诸葛亮是一个杰出的军事家。一次，魏国的将军司马懿带领十五万大军向诸葛亮所在的西城进攻。当时，诸葛亮身边只有二千五百名士兵。听到司马懿带兵前来的消息大家都大惊失色。

诸葛亮不慌不忙地下达命令，叫士兵把城门打开，城门前只派几个兵扮成百姓模样在那儿扫地。诸葛亮自己穿着长袍，带上一张琴，到城楼上坐下，然后慢慢弹起琴来。司马懿到达城下后，看了非常疑惑，就下令撤退。他的助手说："也许诸葛亮手里真的没有兵吧？"司马懿说："诸葛亮一生谨慎，现在城门大开，里面一定有埋伏。还是赶快撤退吧！"司马懿退兵后，诸葛亮才松了一口气，擦掉了额头上的冷汗。

词汇一 VOCABULARY I

蛇	蛇	shé	snake
传	傳	zhuàn	biography, story
计	計	jì	stratagem, scheme, plan
综合	綜合	zōnghé	comprehensive, composite
戏剧	戲劇	xìjù	drama
器乐	器樂	qìyuè	instrumental music
武术	武術	wǔshù	martial arts
化妆	化妝	huàzhuāng	to make up
手段		shǒuduàn	means, way
特色		tèsè	distinctive feature
相貌	相貌	xiàngmào	facial features, looks, appearance
特异	特異	tèyì	peculiar, distinctive
角色	角色	jiǎosè	role, part (in a play, movie, etc.)
脸谱	臉譜	liǎnpǔ	facial design (in Beijing opera)
忠诚	忠誠	zhōngchéng	loyal, faithful
勇猛		yǒngměng	valorous and powerful
凶狠		xiōnghěn	fierce and malicious
暴躁		bàozào	hot tempered
奸诈	奸詐	jiānzhà	crafty and deceitful
剧目	劇目	jùmù	list of plays or operas
自		zì	从
发生	發生	fāshēng	to happen, to take place
娘子		niángzi	lady, wife (in early vernacular)
结成	結成	jiéchéng	to form, to establish
居住		jūzhù	to live
幸福		xìngfú	happy, blissful
和尚		héshàng	Buddhist monk
想方设法	想方設法	xiǎngfāng shèfǎ	to do everything possible, to use all means
拆散		chāisàn	to break up
法术	法術	fǎshù	black magic, supernatural feats
钵	鉢	bō	alms bowl (of a Buddhist monk)
打败	打敗	dǎbài	to defeat (in war)

演义	演義	yǎnyì	historical novel
军事家	軍事家	jūnshìjiā	strategist
将军	將軍	jiāngjūn	general
带领	帶領	dàilǐng	to lead, to guide
士兵		shìbīng	soldier
进攻	進攻	jìngōng	to attack
大惊失色	大驚失色	dàjīng shīsè	to go pale with fear
不慌不忙		bùhuāng bùmáng	unhurriedly, in a leisurely manner
下达	下達	xiàdá	to issue (an order)
命令		mìnglìng	order, command
派		pài	to send, to assign, to appoint
打扮		dǎbàn	to disguise, to make up
百姓		bǎixìng	common people
模样	模樣	múyàng	appearance, look
袍		páo	robe, gown
张	張	zhāng	measure word for the *qin,* paper, etc.
城楼	城樓	chénglóu	gate tower
到达	到達	dàodá	to arrive
疑惑	疑惑	yíhuò	to feel puzzled, to be doubtful
下令	下令	xiàlìng	to give orders
撤退	撤退	chètuì	to retreat
助手		zhùshǒu	assistant
一生		yīshēng	whole life, lifelong
谨慎	謹慎	jǐnshèn	prudent, careful, cautious
松		sōng	to loosen, to relax, to relieve
擦掉	擦掉	cādiào	to wipe
额头	額頭	étóu	forehead
汗		hàn	sweat

专名一 PROPER NAMES I

许仙	許仙	Xǔ Xiān	personal name
西湖		Xīhú	West Lake, in Hangzhou
白娘子		Bái Niángzi	personal name

小青		Xiǎoqīng	personal name
镇江	鎮江	Zhènjiāng	city in Jiangsu Province
金山寺		Jīnshānsì	Jinshan Temple, in Zhenjiang
法海		Fǎhǎi	Buddhist monk
雷峰塔		Léifēngtǎ	Leifeng Pagoda, in Hangzhou
诸葛亮	諸葛亮	Zhūgě Liàng	Shu strategist (181–234)
魏国	魏國	Wèiguó	Kingdom of Wei (220–265)
蜀国	蜀國	Shǔguó	Kingdom of Shu (221–263)
吴国	吳國	Wúguó	Kingdom of Wu (229–280)
司马懿	司馬懿	Sīmǎ Yì	Wei general (179–251)
西城		Xīchéng	in present-day Ankang 安康 City, Shaanxi Province

小故事 Ministory

A Beijing Opera Master in America 大师访美

梅兰芳是中国近代京剧大师。1930年，梅兰芳率剧团赴美演出。半年之中，他们在纽约、芝加哥、旧金山、洛杉矶、华盛顿、西雅图等地公演了七十二场，获得巨大的成功。当时美国正处在经济衰退中，可是在纽约定价六块美金的戏票竟然被卖到四十块。纽约的最后一场演出谢幕之后，梅兰芳站在台前与上台的观众一一握手，握了几十分钟还没完，原来有不少人是握了手以后又来排队的。

在美期间，梅兰芳被南加州大学授予博士学位。他与卓别林等艺术家结下了深厚的友谊。不过有一位美国人没能一饱眼福，他就是胡佛总统。梅兰芳在华盛顿演出时，胡佛恰好在外地。事后胡佛特地打电话邀请梅兰芳再来华盛顿。但由于日程关系，没能成行。为此，梅兰芳和胡佛都觉得非常遗憾。

词汇二 VOCABULARY II

大师	大師	dàshī	master, grand master
访	訪	fǎng	to visit
近代		jìndài	modern times
率		shuài	to lead, to command
剧团	劇團	jùtuán	theatrical company, troupe
赴		fù	to go to, to be bound for
演出	演出	yǎnchū	to perform
公演	公演	gōngyǎn	to perform in public, to give a performance
场	場	chǎng	measure word for movies, plays, concerts, etc.
获得	獲得	huòdé	to get, to gain, to win
巨大		jùdà	tremendous, enormous
成功		chénggōng	success
处在	處在	chùzài	to be (in a certain condition)
衰退		shuāituì	economic recession
定价	定價	dìngjià	fixed price
谢幕	謝幕	xièmù	to take a curtain call
观众	觀眾	guānzhòng	audience
握手		wòshǒu	to shake hands
期间	期間	qījiān	time period
授予		shòuyǔ	to confer, to award
博士		bóshì	doctorate
结下	結下	jiéxià	to form, to forge, to establish
深厚		shēnhòu	deep, profound
友谊	友誼	yǒuyì	friendship
一饱眼福	一飽眼福	yībǎo yǎnfú	to feast one's eyes on something
福		fú	good fortune, luck, blessing, happiness
总统	總統	zǒngtǒng	president (of a state)
恰好		qiàhǎo	by chance, accidentally
邀请	邀請	yāoqǐng	to invite

由于……关系	由於……關係	yóuyú … guānxì	because of, due to
成行		chéngxíng	to be able to go on a trip
遗憾	遺憾	yíhàn	to regret

专名二 PROPER NAMES II

梅兰芳	梅蘭芳	Méi Lánfāng	Beijing opera master (1894–1961)
旧金山		Jiùjīnshān	San Francisco
洛杉矶	洛杉磯	Luòshānjī	Los Angeles
西雅图	西雅圖	Xīyǎtú	Seattle
加州		Jiāzhōu	California
卓别林		Zhuóbiélín	Charlie Chaplin (1889–1977)
胡佛		Húfó	Herbert Clark Hoover (1874–1964)

小知识 Knowledge
Chinese Local Operas 地方戏曲

中国一共有三百多种地方戏曲。很多地方戏是以地名来命名的，比如京剧就是在北京发展起来的。越剧发源于古越国所在地浙江绍兴地区，是仅次于京剧的一个大剧种，代表剧目有《红楼梦》、《梁山伯与祝英台》等。此外，沪剧是上海的地方戏，因为上海简称沪。粤剧是广东省的主要剧种，因为广东简称粤。豫剧是河南省的主要地方戏，因为河南简称豫。

词汇三 VOCABULARY III

地方		dìfāng	locality, local
戏曲	戲曲	xìqǔ	traditional opera
命名		mìngmíng	to name
发源	發源	fāyuán	to originate
地区	地區	dìqū	area, district
仅	僅	jǐn	只, only, merely
次于	次於	cìyú	second to
剧种	劇種	jùzhǒng	type of traditional opera
省		shěng	province

专名三 PROPER NAMES III

绍兴	紹興	Shàoxīng	city in Zhejiang Province
沪	滬	Hù	alternative name for Shanghai
粤		Yuè	alternative name for Guangdong
广东	廣東	Guǎngdōng	Guangdong Province
豫		Yù	alternative name for Henan
河南		Hénán	Henan Province

语言点 Language Points

一、 词语 WORDS

1. 特色 distinctive feature

【课文】京剧的化妆很有特色。

【例句】上海最有特色的小吃就是小笼包了，你吃了沒有？

The most special snack in Shanghai is the "small steamer bun." Have you had it?

2. 表示 to express, to show

【课文】红色的脸谱表示忠诚，黑色的脸谱表示勇猛。

【例句】小张的心情都写在她的脸上：今天她脸上老挂着笑容，就表示她很高兴。

Xiao Zhang's mood is written on her face: today she has a smile on her face, which means she is very happy.

3. 自 from

【课文】京剧的很多剧目改编自历史故事或民间传说。

【例句】我们中文班上有五个同学来自东岸，四个来自西岸，两个来自中西部，还有三个来自亚洲。

Five students in our Chinese class are from the East Coast, four are from the West Coast, two are from the Midwest, and the other three are from Asia.

4. 还是 still, yet, nevertheless

【课文】诸葛亮一生谨慎，现在城门大开，里面必有埋伏。还是赶快撤退吧！

【例句】妈妈虽然已经四十多岁了，但看起来还是很年轻，常常有人說她是我的姐姐呢。

Although Mom is over forty, she still looks very young. People often say she is my older sister.

5. 仅次于 second only to

【课文】越剧发源于古越国所在地浙江绍兴地区，是仅次于京剧的一个大剧种。

【例句】我这次考试的成绩仅次于小王，他是班上唯一及格的人。

My grade on this exam is second only to Xiao Wang's, and he is the only one in the class who passed.

二、句型 SENTENCE PATTERNS

1. V 的是 (emphasizing the object of the verb)

【课文】《空城计》讲的是历史小说《三国演义》中的诸葛亮的故事。

【例句】你以为他在做功课？他现在在电脑上看的是一部爱情电影。

Did you think he was doing homework? Right now he is watching a romantic movie on the computer.

2. V 起 N 来 (describing an action with a slow start or unexpected nature)

【课文】诸葛亮自己穿着长袍，带上一张琴，到城楼上坐下，然后慢慢弹起琴来。

【例句】大家都在认真地上中文课的时候，他却偷偷地睡起觉来。

Everyone is studying seriously in Chinese class, but he dozed off without anyone noticing.

3. 由于……关系 because of, due to

【课文】但由于日程关系，没能成行。

【例句】由于天气关系，他们的登山计划没能实行。

Because of the weather, their plan to climb the mountain could not be realized.

4. 正处在 . . . . . . 之中 in the middle of, in the process of

【课文】当时美国正处在经济衰退中，可是在纽约定价六元美
金的戏票竟然被卖到四十元。

【例句】我现在正处在申请大学的紧张过程之中，哪有心情去
纽约玩儿呢。

I am right in the middle of the tense process of college applications; how
could I be in the mood to visit New York?

5. 可是 . . . . . . 竟然 but . . . unexpectedly

【课文】当时美国正处在经济衰退中，可是在纽约定价六元美
金的戏票竟然被卖到四十元。

【例句】这次网球比赛有很多高手参加，可是冠军竟然被一个
没有名气的、十六岁的小伙子拿走了。

Many masters participated in the tennis competition, but, unexpectedly,
the championship was won by a little-known sixteen-year-old boy.

三、成语 IDIOMS

1. 想方设法 to do everything possible, to use all means

【课文】可是，镇江金山寺的和尚法海想方设法要拆散许仙和
白娘子。

【例句】在这个电脑游戏里，你必须想方设法地把那些敌人全
部消灭了才能赢。

In this computer game, you must try your best to destroy all enemies to
win.

2. 大惊失色 to go pale with fear

【课文】听到司马懿带兵前来的消息大家都大惊失色。

【例句】孙先生回家打开电脑一看大惊失色一股票市场是一片
红色。

Mr. Sun came back home and turned on his computer. He grew pale when
he took a look—the stock markets were all in the red.

3. 不慌不忙 unhurriedly, in a leisurely manner

【课文】诸葛亮不慌不忙地下达命令，叫士兵把城门打开。

【例句】话剧马上就要开始演出了，作为主演的他才不慌不忙
地走进后台。

The play will start soon. As the lead, he came backstage unhurriedly.

4. 一饱眼福 to feast one's eyes on something

【课文】不过有一位美国人没能一饱眼福，他就是胡佛总统。

【例句】今天晚宴的菜都做得那么漂亮，我们不但能一饱口福，还能一饱眼福呢。

All of the dishes at the banquet tonight are so pretty. We can enjoy not only eating them, but also looking at them.

练习 Exercises

一、填名词

Fill in the blanks with appropriate nouns to form adjective-noun phrases.

1. 忠诚的 ＿＿＿ ＿＿＿
2. 勇猛的 ＿＿＿ ＿＿＿
3. 凶狠的 ＿＿＿ ＿＿＿
4. 暴躁的 ＿＿＿ ＿＿＿
5. 奸诈的 ＿＿＿ ＿＿＿
6. 谨慎的 ＿＿＿ ＿＿＿
7. 巨大的 ＿＿＿ ＿＿＿
8. 深厚的 ＿＿＿ ＿＿＿

二、选词填空

Fill in the blanks using the words provided.

（特色、自、表示、还是、仅次于）

1. 你都病成这样了，＿＿＿＿＿＿＿请假一天回家休息吧！
2. 西班牙语在美国也很重要，是 ＿＿＿＿＿＿＿ 英語的第二大语言。
3. 天空这么黑，＿＿＿＿＿＿＿马上要下大雨了。
4. 在我校的国际文化节上，很多学生都穿了有各自的民族 ＿＿＿＿＿＿＿ 的服装。
5. 你帮了我这么多忙，请接受我发 ＿＿＿＿＿＿＿ 内心的感谢。

三、 用句型造句

Compose sentences using the sentence patterns below.

1. V 的是
2. 所 V
3. V 起 N 来
4. 由于……关系
5. 正处在……之中
6. 可是……竟然

四、 用本课的成语改写句子

Rewrite each sentence using idioms you have learned in this lesson.

1. 我因为考试错过了美术展览，艺术大师们的杰作我没能有机会欣赏。
2. 我昨天开上高速公路后吓了一跳，原来我开进对面来车的单行道了。
3. 我知道你的电脑坏了，可是别着急，小孙正在努力帮你修呢。
4. 飞机快要起飞了，大家都往登机口跑去，只有他还在免税店里慢慢地买东西。

五、 选择题

Choose the correct word or phrase to complete each sentence.

1. 性格或相貌上有些 ________ 的男角色，化妆用脸谱，叫"花脸"。
   a. 特异　　　b. 特意
   c. 特出　　　d. 特长
2. 红色的脸谱表示 ________。
   a. 凶狠　　　b. 暴躁
   c. 忠诚　　　d. 奸诈
3. 《空城计》讲的是历史小说《________》中的诸葛亮的故事。
   a. 西游记　　b. 水浒传
   c. 红楼梦　　d. 三国演义

4. 听到司马懿带兵前来的消息大家都 ________。
     a. 面不改色 b. 大惊失色
     c. 不慌不忙 d. 胸有成竹
5. 诸葛亮一生 ________，现在城门大开，里面一定有埋伏。还是
     赶快撤退吧!
     a. 谨慎   b. 忠诚
     c. 勇猛   d. 深厚
6. 梅兰芳是中国 ________ 京剧大师。
     a. 古代   b. 近代
     c. 现代   d. 当代
7. 当时美国正处在经济衰退中，可是在 ________ 定价六元美金的
     戏票竟然被卖到四十元。
     a. 华盛顿   b. 旧金山
     c. 洛杉矶   d. 纽约
8. 广东简称 ________。
     a. 沪   b. 越
     c. 粤   d. 豫

六、改错

Correct the sentences below.

1. 京剧是一门综合的艺术，运用了戏剧、歌唱、器乐、舞蹈、武
     术、化妆等许多技术手段。
2. 《白蛇传》就是一个著名的历史故事。
3. 婚后，许仙和白素贞搬到杭州居住，开了一家药店。
4. 法海用法术将白素贞收入他的钵内，压在西湖边上的金山寺
     下。
5. 唐朝末年，中国分成魏、蜀、吴三国。
6. 一次，吴国的将军司马懿带领十五万大军向诸葛亮所在的西城
     进攻。
7. 诸葛亮自己穿着长袍，带上一个琵琶，到城楼上坐下。
8. 司马懿退兵后，诸葛亮才叹了一口气，擦掉了额头上的冷汗。
9. 在美期间，梅兰芳被加州大学授予博士学位。
10. 事后胡佛特地打电邮邀请梅兰芳再来华盛顿。

七、回答问题

Answer the following questions.

1. 京剧运用了哪些艺术手段？
2. "花脸"的脸谱有哪几种？代表什么样的性格？
3. 许仙在哪里遇见了白素贞？
4. 许仙和白素贞婚后靠什么生活？
5. 为什么诸葛亮要到城楼上去弹琴？
6. 司马懿为什么要退兵？
7. 为什么梅兰芳跟观众握手握了几十分钟还没完？
8. 梅兰芳跟谁结下了深厚的友谊？
9. 胡佛总统为什么没看到梅兰芳的演出？
10. 越剧有哪些代表剧目？

八、英译中

Translate the passages below into Chinese.

1. The West Lake in Hangzhou is not only famous for its picturesque landscape, but it is also associated with many scholars and national heroes—and, thus, encompasses many aspects of Chinese culture. In addition, many ancient buildings, stone caves, and engraved tablets in the surrounding areas are among the most cherished national treasures of China and have significant artistic value.

2. Leifeng Pagoda became a household name in China thanks to the popular folktale *The White Snake.* In the story, the White Snake was finally rescued when the pagoda collapsed. Coincidentally, the pagoda underwent a similar experience in reality. Due to structural damage suffered since the Ming dynasty, the ancient pagoda suddenly collapsed in August 1924. However, the construction of a new Leifeng Pagoda was completed in October 2002.

3. Zhuge Liang was one of the major figures in the historic battle that took place at the Red Cliffs. ① Once, he was assigned to make one hundred thousand arrows in ten days or face execution. Zhuge Liang, however, swore he would finish this seemingly impossible task in three days. He requested twenty large boats, each manned with many straw figures and a few soldiers. Before dawn, Zhuge Liang ordered his soldiers to beat war drums and shout orders

to imitate the noise of an attack. The enemy soldiers, unable to see in the fog, fired many volleys of arrows at the sound of the drums. The straw figures were soon filled with arrows, and Zhuge Liang returned, having fulfilled his promise.

【生词】① Red Cliffs: 赤壁

九、中译英

Translate the passages below into English.

"洋贵妃"

1. 1979年，美国姑娘 Elizabeth Wichmann-Walczak（中文名叫魏莉莎）来到南京大学学习汉语和戏剧。魏莉莎同时到江苏省京剧院学习京剧。她拜戏剧大师梅兰芳的嫡传弟子沈小梅为师，每天清晨与京剧演员一起练嗓子和基本功。

2. 在沈小梅的精心指导下，魏莉莎学了梅派名剧《贵妃醉酒》。1981年春天，魏莉莎在南京大学礼堂举行了《贵妃醉酒》的首场汇报演出。她扮相俊美、唱腔圆润，将杨贵妃醉酒时复杂而矛盾的心理刻画得细致入微、逼真传神，被人们亲切地称为"洋贵妃"。

3. 魏丽莎后来担任美国夏威夷大学戏剧舞蹈系教授，并成为用英文表演京剧的首创者。1986年，魏莉莎翻译并导演的第一部英语京剧《凤还巢》在夏威夷上演，反响热烈。以后她又指导她的学生排了很多京剧大戏，在美国和中国演出。演员们穿着京剧戏服，唱、念、做、打，一丝不苟，每场都赢得观众的热烈鼓掌和阵阵叫好。如果梅兰芳知道有这样一个再传弟子在美国推广京剧，一定会很高兴的。

九、故事复述

Retell the following stories:

1. 白蛇传
2. 空城计

十、课堂辩论

Debate the question posed below.

【题目】京剧有前途吗？

【提示】正方：真正的艺术是会代代相传的。的确，要欣赏京剧要有很多知识，所以观众里中、老年人较多。但现在的年轻人也会变老，那时就会从摇滚乐转向京剧了。反方：你要读过《水浒传》，才能欣赏《武松打虎》；读过《三国演义》，才能欣赏《空城计》，多不容易啊。老是演古代的人，年轻人怎么会喜欢呢？

十一、作文

Write a short composition of approximately three hundred characters on the topic below.

【题目】许仙值得白素贞爱吗？

【提示】在中文或英文的网站上看一下《白蛇传》的故事，再回答这个问题。要用具体例子来说明你的看法。

十二、专题研究

Research the topics below online and report to the class.

1. 讲一个比较完整的《白蛇传》的故事。
2. 讲一下诸葛亮《借东风》的故事。

IDIOMS 成语

Awaiting the Hare under the Tree and
Swordplay at the Rooster's Crow
守株待兔与闻鸡起舞

　　成语是语言中经过长期使用而形成的固定短语。成语一般用四个字，生动简洁，又能表达丰富的意思。汉语历史悠久，成语也特别多。大部分成语是从古代沿用下来的，背后往往有一个寓言故事或历史故事。

　　"守株待兔"这句成语就是一个寓言故事。春秋时期有个农夫。一天，他在地里干活，忽然看见一只兔子箭一般地飞奔过来，撞在一棵大树上，一下子就死了。农夫把兔子捡起来，高兴地说："这真是得来全不费工夫，回去可以美美地吃上一顿了。"他提着兔子一边往家走，一边得意地想："我的运气真好，说不定明天还会有兔子跑来，我可不能放过这样的机会。"

　　第二天，他到地里，也不干活，只守着那棵大树。结果，等了一天什么也没等到。他却不甘心，从此，天天坐在那棵大树下等着兔子来撞死。他等呀等呀，直等到地里的野草长得比庄稼都高了，一个兔子都没看到。

　　"闻鸡起舞"讲的是一个历史故事。晋代的祖逖和好友刘琨年轻时住在一个屋子里，用功读书。一次，祖逖在睡梦中听到雄鸡的鸣叫声，他把刘琨叫醒，说："报晓鸡已经叫了，我们起床练剑，好吗？"刘琨听了，翻身起床。两人走到院子里，在月光下练剑，一直练到朝霞满天才收剑。从此，春去秋来，寒来暑往，从不间断。经过长期的训练，他们终于成为能文能武的全才。

　　"闻鸡起舞"讲的是一种积极的人生态度，"守株待兔"则是一种消极的生活方式。正反两方面的成语都非常多，再举几个例子。"画龙点睛"是有效的努力，"画蛇添足" 就是做了多余的事。成语用来讽刺、批评的也很多。如 "对牛弹琴" 的是傻瓜，"狐假虎威" 的是小人，"口蜜腹剑" 是奸诈、"掩耳盗铃" 是自欺、"螳臂挡车" 是不自量力。这些成语，虽然看了就知道它们的意思，但背后也都有一个故事。你能到网上去查一下吗？

词汇一 VOCABULARY I

守		shǒu	to keep watch, to look after
株		zhū	trunk, stump
待		dài	等
兔		tù	hare, rabbit
经过	經過	jīngguò	having gone through, after
固定		gùdìng	fixed
短语	短語	duǎnyǔ	phrase
简洁	簡潔	jiǎnjié	succinct
悠久		yōujiǔ	long, age-old
沿用		yányòng	to continue to use (an old method, etc.)
寓言		yùyán	fable
农夫	農夫	nóngfū	peasant, farmer
干活	幹活	gànhuó	to work on a job, to do manual labor
忽然		hūrán	suddenly
箭		jiàn	arrow
奔		bēn	to run, to rush, to dash
撞		zhuàng	to bump against, to crash
捡	撿	jiǎn	to pick up
费	費	fèi	to cost, to spend
提		tí	to carry (in hand with arm hanging down)
得意		déyì	self-satisfied
运气	運氣	yùnqì	luck
说不定	說不定	shuōbúdìng	perhaps, possibly
放过	放過	fàngguò	to let slip by
甘心		gānxīn	to be willing to, to resign oneself to

野草		yěcǎo	weeds
庄稼	莊稼	zhuāngjia	crops
雄		xióng	male (animal)
鸣	鳴	míng	bird's cry
报晓	報曉	bàoxiǎo	to be a harbinger of dawn
剑	劍	jiàn	sword
翻身		fānshēn	to turn over
朝霞		zhāoxiá	rosy clouds of dawn
间断	間斷	jiānduàn	to be interrupted
训练	訓練	xùnliàn	training
全才		quáncái	person of many talents
积极	積極	jījí	positive
态度	態度	tàidù	attitude
则	則	zé	but, however
消极	消極	xiāojí	negative
正反		zhèngfǎn	positive and negative, both sides
举例子	舉例子	jǔlìzǐ	to give examples
点	點	diǎn	to dot
有效		yǒuxiào	effective
努力		nǔlì	effort
讽刺	諷刺	fěngcì	to satirize
傻瓜		shǎguā	fool, idiot
狐（狸）		hú(lí)	fox
假		jiǎ	借
虎		hǔ	tiger
威		wēi	prowess, might
小人		xiǎorén	mean person
蜜		mì	honey
掩		yǎn	to cover, to conceal
盗		dào	to steal
铃	鈴	líng	bell
欺		qī	to cheat, to deceive
螳		táng	mantis

臂		bì	arm
挡	擋	dǎng	to keep off, to get in the way of
不自量力		bùzì liànglì	to overrate one's own abilities
网	網	wǎng	World Wide Web, the Internet

专名一 PROPER NAMES I

祖逖	祖逖	Zǔ Tì	Jin general (266–321)
刘琨	劉琨	Liú Kūn	Jin general (271–318)

小故事 Ministory

Southbound Carriage, Northbound Tracks 南辕北辙

战国时，魏国的国王想出兵攻打赵国。大臣季梁本来已出使邻国，听到这个消息，立刻半途返回，去见魏王，劝他不要攻打赵国。

季梁对魏王说："今天我在路上，遇见一个人坐车朝北去，但他告诉我要到楚国去。楚国在南方，我问他为什么去南方反而朝北走？那人说：'不要紧，我的马好，跑得快。'我提醒他，马好也没用，朝北不是到楚国该走的方向。那人指着车上的大口袋说：'不要紧，我的路费多着呢。'我又跟他说，路费多也没用，这样到不了楚国。那人还是说：'不要紧，我的车夫最会赶车。'这人真是太糊涂了，他的方向不对，即使马跑得特别快，路费带得特别多，车夫特别会赶车，也没用。这些条件越好，也只能使他离开目的地越远。"

接着，季梁说到本题："大王要当各国的领袖，一举一动都要作出榜样；如果仗着自己国家大、兵力强去进攻别国，这就不能建立威信。这就像那个要去楚国的人一样，南辕北辙，只能离您的目标越来越远！"魏王被季梁说服了，决定停止攻打赵国。

词汇二 VOCABULARY II

辕	轅	yuán	shafts (of a cart, etc.)
辙	轍	zhé	track (of a vehicle), rut
攻打		gōngdǎ	to attack, to assault
大臣		dàchén	minister, courtier
本来		běnlái	originally
出使		chūshǐ	to serve as an envoy abroad, to be sent on a diplomatic mission
立刻		lìkè	immediately
半途		bàntú	halfway
返回		fǎnhuí	to return
朝		cháo	向，往
反而		fǎn'ér	on the contrary, instead
提醒		tíxǐng	to remind
方向		fāngxiàng	direction
要紧	要緊	yàojǐn	important, serious, urgent
车夫	車夫	chēfū	driver (of a carriage)
赶车	趕車	gǎnchē	to drive a cart or carriage
糊涂	糊塗	hútú	muddled, confused
条件	條件	tiáojiàn	condition, circumstance
目的地		mùdìdì	destination
本题		běntí	point at issue, subject under discussion
领袖	領袖	lǐngxiù	leader
榜样	榜樣	bǎngyàng	good example, role model
仗着	仗著	zhàngzhe	to rely on, on the strength of, due to
威信		wēixìn	prestige, power, popularity
目标	目標	mùbiāo	goal
说服	說服	shuōfú	to persuade, to convince

专名二 PROPER NAMES II

战国	戰國	Zhànguó	Warring States period (475–221 BCE)
魏国	魏國	Wèiguó	State of Wei (403–225 BCE)
赵国	趙國	Zhàoguó	State of Zhao (403–222 BCE)
季梁	季梁	Jìliáng	personal name

小知识 Knowledge
Proverbs and Riddles 谚语谜语

谚语是流传于民间的语句，常常能使语言活泼风趣，增强文章的表现力。

有的谚语是单句的，如：家和万事兴；无风不起浪；百闻不如一见；失败是成功之母。

有些谚语是两句的。有四字句的，如：病从口入，祸从口出；千里之行，始于足下。有五字句的，如：在家靠父母，出门靠朋友；人往高处走，水往低处流。有六字句的，如：天有不测风云，人有旦夕祸福；远水不解近渴，远亲不如近邻。有七字句的，如：一年之计在于春，一日之计在于晨；车到山前必有路，船到桥头自会直。

谜语是一种文字游戏，猜谜语需要一定的知识，也很有趣。一条谜语包含谜面、谜目和谜底三个部分。谜面好比是题目，谜底是答案，谜目是答案的范围。比如，"凤头虎尾"作谜面，"打一字"是谜目，谜底是"几"字，因为凤字的"头"和"虎"字的"尾"都是个"几"字。

字谜是谜语的一种，就是谜底是个字。这里举些简单的字谜例子。所有这些谜语都是打一个字，所以谜目就省略了。谜底就放在括号里，你不用猜。但是你要告诉老师，为什么是这个谜底呢？

一加一 （王）、十加十 （茄）、十五天（胖）、十月十日（朝）、舌头（千）、火腿（人）、可上可下（哥）、见人就笑（竺）、谢绝参观（企）、七十二小时（晶）。

词汇三 VOCABULARY III

谚语	諺語	yànyǔ	proverb, saying
谜语	謎語	míyǔ	riddle
流传	流傳	liúchuán	to circulate, to hand down
活泼	活潑	huópō	lively
风趣	風趣	fēngqù	humorous

增强		zēngqiáng	to strengthen
兴	興	xīng	to rise, to flourish
浪		làng	wave
失败	失敗	shībài	failure
祸	禍	huò	misfortune, disaster
不测		bùcè	unpredictable
旦夕		dànxī	dawn and dusk—imminent
解		jiě	to relieve
谜底	謎底	mídǐ	answer to a riddle
谜面	謎面	mímiàn	riddle
谜目	謎目	mímù	clue to a riddle
范围	範圍	fànwéi	scope, range
打		dǎ	to guess (the answer to a riddle)
省略		shěnglüè	to omit
括号	括號	kuòhào	parenthesis, bracket
茄		qié	eggplant
胖		pàng	fat, plump
企		qǐ	to stand on tiptoe, to look forward to
晶		jīng	brilliant, glittering
谢绝	謝絕	xièjué	to decline politely

专名三 PROPER NAMES III

竺	Zhú	surname

语言点 Language Points

一、词语 WORDS

1. 大部分 majority

【课文】汉语历史悠久，成语也特别多。大部分成语是从古代沿用下来的。

【例句】中国人口众多，有五十六个民族，但大部分是汉族人。

China has a large population, with fifty-six ethnic groups. However, the majority are Han people.

2. 忽然 suddenly

【课文】一天，他在地里干活，忽然看见一只兔子箭一般地飞奔过来。

【例句】小高对中文一直　没兴趣，这学期却忽然决定　修一门中文课，大概是因为他有了一个中国女朋友了。

Xiao Gao has never been interested in Chinese, but he suddenly decided to take a Chinese class this semester. This is probably because he now has a Chinese girlfriend.

3. 说不定 perhaps, possibly

【课文】我的运气真好，说不定明天还会有兔子跑来。

【例句】不要再为学费发愁了，说不定你今天买的彩票会中奖呢？

Don't worry about the tuition anymore. Perhaps you will win the lottery with the ticket you bought today.

4. 靠 to lean on, to be close to, to depend on

【课文】在家靠父母，出门靠朋友。

【例句】这个地方三面环水，一面靠山，风景特别优美。

This place is surrounded by water on three sides and is close to a mountain on the other; the scenery is especially beautiful.

5. 反而 on the contrary, instead

【课文】我问他为什么去南方反而朝北走？

【例句】你考试前天天开夜车，身体累坏了，反而考不好。

You work late into the night every day before your exams. However, you will not do well if you wear yourself out.

6. 仗着 to rely on, on the strength of, due to

【课文】如果仗着自己国家大、兵力强去进攻别国，这就不能建立威信。

【例句】小金仗着家里有钱，对别人很不客气，结果没人愿意跟他交朋友。

Xiao Jin relies on his wealthy family and is not polite to other people. As a result, nobody wants to be friends with him.

二、句型 SENTENCE PATTERNS

1. V 呀 V 呀 (emphasizing the long duration of an action and anxiety while doing it)

【课文】他等呀等呀，直等到地里的野草长得比庄稼都高了，一个兔子都没看到。

【例句】他盼呀盼呀，总算盼到了北大的录取通知书，他的梦想实现了。

He waited anxiously for a long time, and finally got a letter of admission to Beijing University. His dream came true.

2. 比……都…… (describing something as superlative)

【课文】他等呀等呀，直等到地里的野草长得比庄稼都高了，一个兔子都没看到。

【例句】看到孩子们成家立业，父母亲会觉得比什么都高兴。

Parents feel happiest when they see their children with families and careers of their own.

3. 经过……终于…… through . . . finally

【课文】经过长期的训练，他们终于成为能文能武的全才。

【例句】经过这次的失败，他终于明白了做事要脚踏实地，不能一步登天。

Having gone through this failure, he finally understood that he needs to have his feet planted on solid ground and not expect to reach heaven in a single bound.

4. 是……则是 (describing two different things)

【课文】"闻鸡起舞"讲的是一种积极的人生态度，"守株待兔"则是一种消极的生活方式。

【例句】北京是中国的政治中心，上海则是中国的经济中心。

Beijing is China's political center, and Shanghai its economic center.

5. ……的是…… (presenting a verb-object structure as a noun)

【课文】"对牛弹琴"的是傻瓜，"狐假虎威"的是小人。

【例句】你一看就知道了：穿西装的是教授，穿汗衫的是学生。

You can tell at a glance: those in suits are professors and those in t-shirts are students.

6. 即使……也 even if

　　【课文】即使马跑得特别快，路费带得特别多，马夫特别会赶车，也没用。

　　【例句】即使我今晚不睡觉，这篇论文也写不好了，你说我怎么办呢？

Even if I don't sleep tonight I will not finish this essay. Tell me what I should do.

三、成语 IDIOMS

1. 画蛇添足 to draw a snake with feet, to gild the lily

　　【课文】"画龙点睛"是有效的努力，"画蛇添足"就是做了多余的事。

　　【例句】你穿这件大衣很好看，可是如果再戴这条围巾，就是画蛇添足了。

You look good in this coat, but if you also wear the scarf it would be gilding the lily.

2. 对牛弹琴 to play the zither to a cow, to cast pearls before swine

　　【课文】如"对牛弹琴"的是傻瓜，"狐假虎威"的是小人，"口蜜腹剑"是奸诈、"掩耳盗铃"是自欺欺人、"螳臂挡车" 是不自量力。

　　【例句】你跟我这个不懂音乐的人大谈贝多芬，简直是对牛弹琴嘛！

You talk at length to me, who knows nothing about music, about Beethoven. It's like playing the zither to a cow!

3. 狐假虎威 the fox assumes the tiger's awe (by walking in the latter's company), to swagger about in borrowed plumes

　　【课文】同上。

　　【例句】她不过是个总经理助理，可是每天狐假虎威，比总经理更像总经理。

She is merely an assistant to the CEO, but, like the fox assuming the tiger's awe, she looks more like a CEO than the CEO himself.

4. 掩耳盗铃 to plug one's ears while stealing a bell, to practice self-deception

　　【课文】同上。

【例句】小李整天玩电脑游戏，虽然他关上了房门，但是音乐这么响，父母怎么会不知道？真是掩耳盗铃，自欺欺人。

Xiao Li plays computer games all day long. Although he closes the door, the music is so loud; how could his parents not know? He is plugging his ears while stealing a bell—deluding himself.

5. 南辕北辙 to try to go south but drive the chariot north, to act in a way that defeats one's purpose

【课文】这就像那个要去楚国的人一样，南辕北辙，只能离您的目标越来越远！

【例句】你的专业是商业，　可是你修的课都是文学，那不是南辕北辙吗？什么时候才能毕业？

Your major is business, but the courses you are taking are all literature courses—doesn't that defeat the purpose? When will you be able to graduate?

练习 Exercises

一、填名词

Fill in the blanks with appropriate nouns to form adjective-noun phrases.

1. 生动的 ＿＿＿＿ ＿＿＿＿
2. 简洁的 ＿＿＿＿ ＿＿＿＿
3. 丰富的 ＿＿＿＿ ＿＿＿＿
4. 悠久的 ＿＿＿＿ ＿＿＿＿
5. 得意的 ＿＿＿＿ ＿＿＿＿
6. 长期的 ＿＿＿＿ ＿＿＿＿
7. 有效的 ＿＿＿＿ ＿＿＿＿
8. 多余的 ＿＿＿＿ ＿＿＿＿
9. 糊涂的 ＿＿＿＿ ＿＿＿＿
10. 活泼的 ＿＿＿＿ ＿＿＿＿
11. 风趣的 ＿＿＿＿ ＿＿＿＿
12. 有趣的 ＿＿＿＿ ＿＿＿＿
13. 简单的 ＿＿＿＿ ＿＿＿＿

二、选词填空

Fill in the blanks using the words provided.

（大部分、忽然、说不定、靠、反而、仗着）

1. 她上大学不 ________ 爸爸妈妈，用自己在饭店打工赚的钱付学费。
2. 你从小喜欢数学，现在却是个艺术家；他数学一直很差，现在 ________ 在读数学博士。
3. 她 ________ 自己是城里人，就看不起那些从乡下来的同学。
4. 虽然他很喜欢打电脑游戏，但 ________ 的时间还是花在了学习上面。
5. 看完那封信后，他 ________ 脸色一变，气冲冲地跑出去了。
6. 你别看我现在游泳游得 不快，________ 有一天我会打破世界纪录呢。

三、用句型造句

Compose sentences using the sentence patterns below.

1. V 呀 V 呀
2. 比 …… 都 ……
3. 经过 …… 终于 ……
4. 是 … 则是
5. …… 的是 ……
6. 即使 …… 也

四、用本课的成语改写句子

Rewrite each sentence using idioms you have learned in this lesson.

1. 我们要去中央公园， 公共汽车应该往北开，可是这辆车是往南开的，这不是方向错了吗！
2. 你可不能仗着你的朋友会功夫，就到处欺负人啊！
3. 他根本就没有在听，所以你刚刚的那些话算是白讲了。
4. 你的这篇文章已经写得很完整了，如果再加上这一段话，就是多余的了。

五、选择题

Choose the correct word or phrase to complete each sentence.

1. 成语是语言中经过长期使用而形成的 ________ 短语。
   a. 固定　　b. 一定
   c. 必定　　d. 决定

2. 大部分成语是从古代 ________ 下来的。
   a. 使用　　b. 沿用
   c. 应用　　d. 运用

3. "守株待兔"这句成语就是一个 ________ 故事。
   a. 历史　　b. 神话
   c. 寓言　　d. 民间

4. 他拎着兔子一边往家走，一边 ________ 地想："我的运气真好。"
   a. 满意　　b. 乐意
   c. 愿意　　d. 得意

5. "闻鸡起舞"讲的是一种积极的人生 ________。
   a. 方式　　b. 办法
   c. 态度　　d. 习惯

6. "对牛弹琴"的是 ________。
   a. 傻瓜　　b. 坏蛋
   c. 小人　　d. 奸人

7. 楚国在 ________ 方。
   a. 东　　　b. 南
   c. 西　　　d. 北

8. 不要紧，我的 ________ 多着呢。
   a. 路费　　b. 车费
   c. 运费　　d. 小费

9. 不要紧，我的马夫最会 ________ 车。
   a. 开　　　b. 拉
   c. 骑　　　d. 赶

10. 猜 ________ 需要一定的知识，也很有趣。
    a. 谜语　　b. 谜面
    c. 谜底　　d. 谜目

六、改错

Correct the sentences below.

1. 汉代的祖逖和好友刘琨年轻时住在一个屋子里，用功读书。
2. 两人走到院子里，在月光下练剑，一直练到晚霞满天才收剑。
3. "画蛇添足"是有效的努力。
4. "掩耳盗铃"是不自量力。
5. 战国时，秦国的国王想出兵攻打赵国。
6. 季梁在路上遇见一个人坐车朝南去。
7. 他的目的不对，即使马跑得特别快，也没用。

七、回答问题

Answer the questions below.

1. 什么是成语？
2. 成语一般用几个字？
3. 为什么汉语中成语特别多？
4. 农夫坐在树下等什么？
5. "守株待兔"这句成语说明了什么？
6. 季梁为什么要跟魏王讲"南辕北辙"的故事？
7. 什么是谚语？

八、英译中

Translate the passages below into Chinese.

1. Chinese idioms in isolation are often unintelligible to modern Chinese people, and when students in China learn idioms, they also need to study the contexts from which the idioms were born. Often the four characters reflect the moral behind a story rather than the story itself. For example, the phrase 破釜沉舟 literally means, "to break the woks and sink the boats." It was based on a historical account in which General Xiang Yu 项羽 ordered his troops to destroy all cooking utensils and boats after crossing a river into enemy territory. He won the battle because of this "no-retreat" strategy. Similar phrases are known in the West, such as "burning one's bridges" or "crossing the Rubicon." This particular idiom cannot be used in a losing scenario because the story behind it does not describe a failure.

2. Another example is 瓜田李下, which literally means "in a melon field and under the plum trees." It is an idiom with a deeper meaning that implies suspicious situations. It is derived from a poem from the Han dynasty. The poem contains two phrases: 瓜田不納履，李下不整冠, which describe a code of conduct that says, "Don't adjust your shoes in a melon field and don't tidy your hat under the plum trees" in order to avoid suspicion of stealing. The literal meaning of the idiom is impossible to understand without knowledge of its origin.

九、中英译

Translate the proverbs below into English.

1. 人无远虑，必有近忧
2. 逆水行舟，不进则退
3. 不听老人言，吃苦在眼前
4. 留得青山在，不怕没柴烧
5. 路遥知马力，日久见人心
6. 世上无难事，只怕有心人
7. 一回被蛇咬，十年怕草绳
8. 只要功夫深，铁杵磨成针
9. 画人画虎难画骨，知人知面难知心
10. 一寸光阴一寸金，寸金难买寸光阴

十、故事复述

Retell the following stories:

1. 守株待兔
2. 闻鸡起舞
3. 南辕北辙

十一、猜字谜

Explain the riddles below.

1. 十个哥哥 （克）
2. 次子（元）
3. 客满（促）

4. 夕（晒）
5. 枯泉（白）
6. 一字十八点（术）

十二、成语故事

Describe the origins of the two idioms below.
1. 拔苗助长
2. 刻舟求剑

HOLIDAYS 节日

Chang'e Flying to the Moon and
Reunion on the Magpie Bridge
嫦娥奔月与鹊桥相会

　　中国有很多传统节日，最主要的当然是中国新年，也叫春节。其他重要的节日还有中秋节、端午节和清明节等。

　　中秋节是仅次于春节的第二大传统节日。农历八月十五日是中秋节。按照农历，七、八、九三个月是秋天。八月十五正在秋天的正中，所以叫中秋节。农历每月十五日是圆月。人们把圆月当作团圆的象征，把中秋节作为亲人团聚的日子。中秋夜，家家户户在一起赏月和品尝月饼。

　　在月饼盒上，常常能看到一个仙女的形象，这就是嫦娥，中国的月亮女神。"嫦娥奔月"是一个有名的神话故事。相传嫦娥在吃了不死药后，飞到天上，成了月亮上的仙女。人们在望月时，常会说月亮上的一块阴影是嫦娥的身影。

　　在初秋，农历七月初七的晚上，人们还会仰望星空，讲着"鹊桥相会"的传说。

　　周朝时有一贫苦青年，叫牛郎，整天与一条老黄牛相伴。老黄牛原来是天上的神仙下凡。一天，老黄牛给牛郎带来一位美丽的姑娘，她是天上的织女，下凡来到人间。织女看到忠厚的牛郎就爱上了他，并答应嫁给他。婚后，他们男耕女织，相亲相爱。织女还生了一男一女两个可爱的孩子。

　　不料，织女私自下凡的事被王母娘娘知道了，派天兵天将把她抓回宫里。牛郎把两个孩子放入箩筐中，一肩挑起，去找织女。在老黄牛的帮助下，他飞到了天上。眼看织女就在面前，却被王母娘娘察觉了。她拔下头上的金钗，在牛郎与织女之间一划，立刻出现了一条波涛汹涌的银河。从此两人一个河西，一个河东，无法相会。他们的忠贞爱情感动了喜鹊。在农历七月初七的晚上，成千上万只喜鹊飞来，口尾连接，搭起一座鹊桥，让牛郎织女走上鹊桥相会。王母娘娘也只好允许两人在每年七月七日在鹊桥相会一次。

后来，每到七月初七，人们就会仰望星空。在秋夜的繁星中，人们会看到银河两边有两颗较大的星星，那就是织女星和牵牛星。和牵牛星在一起的还有两颗小星星，那就是牛郎织女的一儿一女。这样就形成了七夕节。现在，很多人把这个日子作为中国的情人节。

词汇一 VOCABULARY I

鹊	鵲	què	magpie
桥	橋	qiáo	bridge
相会	相會	xiānghuì	to meet each other
团聚	團聚	tuánjù	reunion
团	團	tuán	round, circular
品尝	品嘗	pǐncháng	to taste, to savor, to sample
盒		hé	box, case
仙女		xiānnǚ	celestial lady, goddess
形象		xíngxiàng	image
神		shén	god
神话	神話	shénhuà	mythology
相传	相傳	xiāngchuán	according to legend
块	塊	kuài	measure word for something cubical or flat in shape
阴影	陰影	yīnyǐng	shadow
身影		shēnyǐng	a person's silhouette, figure
仰望	仰望	yǎngwàng	to look upward
星空	星空	xīngkōng	starry sky
黄牛		huángniú	ox
相伴		xiāngbàn	to accompany each other
下凡		xiàfán	(of gods or immortals) to descend to the world
织	織	zhī	to weave
忠厚		zhōnghòu	honest and sincere

耕	耕	gēng	to plow, to till, to farm
不料		bùliào	unexpectedly
私自		sīzì	secretly, without permission
天兵天将	天兵天將	tiānbīng tiānjiāng	soldiers and generals from heaven
抓		zhuā	to catch, to arrest
宫	宮	gōng	palace
箩筐	籮筐	luókuāng	large bamboo or wicker basket
肩	肩	jiān	shoulder
挑		tiāo	to carry on the shoulder with a pole
察觉	察覺	chájué	to become aware of, to discover
金钗		jīnchāi	golden hairpin
之间	之間	zhījiān	between, among
划	劃	huá	to slice
波涛	波濤	bōtāo	waves
汹涌	洶湧	xiōngyǒng	surging, turbulent
忠贞	忠貞	zhōngzhēn	loyal and staunch
喜鹊	喜鵲	xǐquè	magpie
连接	連接	liánjiē	to join, to link
搭		dā	to put up, to build
座		zuò	measure word for houses, bridges, etc.
允许	允許	yǔnxǔ	to allow, to permit
繁		fán	many, numerous
牵	牽	qiān	to lead, to pull

专名一 PROPER NAMES I

嫦娥		Cháng'é	Goddess of the Moon
中秋节	中秋節	Zhōngqiū jié	Mid-Autumn Festival, Moon Festival
端午节	端午節	Duānwǔ jié	Dragon Boat Festival
清明节	清明節	Qīngmíng jié	Tomb-Sweeping Day
牛郎		Niúláng	Cowherd
织女	織女	Zhīnǚ	Weaver
王母娘娘		Wángmǔ niángniáng	Queen Mother of the Western Heavens, a figure in Daoist mythology

银河		Yínhé	Milky Way
织女星	織女星	Zhīnǚ xīng	Vega (star)
牵牛星	牽牛星	Qiānniú xīng	Altair (star)
七夕	七夕	Qīxī	seventh evening of the seventh lunar month
情人节	情人節	Qíngrén jié	Valentine's Day, Sweethearts' Day

小故事 Ministory
A Drowned Poet 屈原沉江

农历五月初五是端午节，人们要吃粽子和赛龙舟。据说，这些都是为了纪念诗人屈原。

在战国时期，中国分成七个国家。其中最强大的是秦、楚、齐三国。屈原是楚国的大臣，他主张改革政治，联齐抗秦。但由于受到小人的诽谤，屈原被流放到边远地区。在流放期间，屈原写了很多诗，表达自己内心的痛苦和对楚国忠贞的感情。公元前278年，秦军南下，攻破了楚国首都。农历五月初五，屈原满腔悲愤，沉江自杀。

人们听到屈原沉江的消息，立刻划船捞救，此后逐渐发展成为赛龙舟的活动。人们又把米饭塞在竹筒里，放到江中给屈原吃，这成了粽子的起源。

词汇二 VOCABULARY II

沉		chén	to sink
纪念	紀念	jìniàn	to commemorate
主张	主張	zhǔzhāng	to advocate
政治		zhèngzhì	politics, political affairs
联	聯	lián	to ally
抗		kàng	to resist, to fight against
受到		shòudào	to sustain, to suffer
诽谤	誹謗	fěibàng	slander
流放		liúfàng	exile

内心		nèixīn	heart, the bottom of one's heart
感情		gǎnqíng	feeling, emotion
南下		nánxià	to go down south
攻破		gōngpò	to break through, to breach
满腔		mǎnqiāng	(with one's heart) filled with, full of
悲愤	悲憤	bēifèn	grief
死讯	死訊	sǐxùn	news of somebody's death
划	劃	huá	to paddle, to row
捞	撈	lāo	to take out of the water, to dredge up, to scoop up
逐渐	逐漸	zhújiàn	gradually
塞		sāi	to fill, to stuff
起源	起源	qǐyuán	origin

专名二 PROPER NAMES II

| 屈原 | | Qū Yuán | China's earliest great poet (ca. 340–ca. 278 BCE) |
| 齐国 | 齊國 | Qíguó | State of Qi |

小知识 Knowledge

Chinese New Year Traditions 春节习俗

　　农历正月初一是中国新年，也叫春节，是中国最隆重、最富有特色的传统节日。

　　除夕夜，全家人在一起吃年夜饭。菜很丰盛，菜名还往往有吉祥的寓意。比如热气腾腾的火锅，说明红红火火；又如"鱼"和"余"谐音，象征"年年有余"。吃了年夜饭，孩子们要到院子里去放爆竹，一直放到午夜以后，表示辞旧迎新。

　　初一早饭要吃年糕，象征"年年高"；还要吃汤圆，寓意"团团圆圆"。然后全家一起出去到长辈和亲朋好友家中去祝贺新年，叫"拜年"。拜年时，长辈往往要给小孩一些钱，放在一个红包里，叫"压岁钱"。古时候春节节庆活动要到正月十五元宵节才结束，现在一般会持续三天。

　　现代春节习俗也有很多改变。除夕家家户户都一边吃年夜饭，一边看电视里的春节晚会的节目。随着科技的发展，出现了新的拜年形式，如电话拜年、手机短信拜年、网上拜年等。

词汇三 VOCABULARY III

习俗	習俗	xísú	custom
正月		zhēngyuè	first month of the lunar year
初一		chūyī	first day of a lunar month
隆重	隆重	lóngzhòng	grand, ceremonious
富有		fùyǒu	rich in, replete with, full of
年夜饭	年夜飯	niányèfàn	New Year's Eve dinner
丰盛	豐盛	fēngshèng	lavish, sumptuous
吉祥		jíxiáng	lucky, auspicious
寓意		yùyì	implied meaning, moral, message
热气腾腾	熱氣騰騰	rèqì téngténg	steaming hot
火锅	火鍋	huǒguō	hotpot
红火	紅火	hónghuǒ	flourishing, prosperous
余	餘	yú	surplus, remainder
谐音	諧音	xiéyīn	homophonic
放		fàng	to set off (a firecracker)
爆竹		bàozhú	firecracker
午夜		wǔyè	midnight
辞旧迎新	辭舊迎新	cíjiù yíngxīn	to bid farewell to the old and usher in the new
年糕		niángāo	New Year cake (made of glutinous rice flour)
长辈	長輩	zhǎngbèi	senior member of a family, person of the elder generation
祝贺	祝賀	zhùhè	to congratulate
拜年		bàinián	to pay a New Year call
拜		bài	to do obeisance, to bow, to kowtow
红包		hóngbāo	red envelope containing money
持续	持續	chíxù	to continue, to sustain
科技		kējì	science and technology

专名三 PROPER NAMES III

元宵节	元宵節	Yuánxiāo jié	Lantern Festival

语言点 Language Points

一、　词语 WORDS

1. 当然 certainly, of course
   【课文】中国有很多传统节日，最主要的当然是中国新年。
   【例句】既然我们到了北京，当然要去吃一顿北京烤鸭。
   Since we are in Beijing now, of course we should eat Beijing duck.

2. 其他 other, else
   【课文】其他重要的节日还有中秋节、端午节和清明节等。
   【例句】让老人和小孩先上车，其他的人请等下一辆车。
   Let the elders and children get on the bus first. Everyone else please wait
   for the next bus.

3. 原来 so, as it turns out
   【课文】老黄牛原来是天上的神仙下凡。
   【例句】他睡了十五个小时后才发现原来睡得太久人反而会更
   累。
   After sleeping for fifteen hours, he realized that sleeping too long actually
   makes people feel even more tired.

4. 不料 unexpectedly
   【课文】不料，织女私自下凡的事被王母娘娘知道了，派天兵
   天将把她抓回宫里。
   【例句】他去年大学毕业，不料经济危机爆发，结果连工作都
   找不到。
   He graduated from college last year. The economic crisis occurred
   unexpectedly. As a result, he could not even find a job.

5. 据说 it is said, reportedly
   【课文】农历五月初五是端午节，人们要吃粽子和赛龙舟。据
   说，这些都是为了纪念诗人屈原。
   【例句】王西之先生写起字来龙飞凤舞，据说他是王羲之的第
   五十六代子孙呢。
   Mr. Wang Xizhi's calligraphy is lively and vibrant. It is said that he is a
   fifty-sixth-generation descendent of Wang Xizhi.

6. 随着 along with, following

【课文】随着科技的发展，出现了新的拜年形式，如电话拜年、手机短信拜年、网上拜年等。

【例句】随着中国经济的快速发展，我校学中文的学生越来越多了。

With the rapid development of China's economy, there have been more and more students of Chinese language at our university.

二、句型 SENTENCE PATTERNS

1. 把……当作（把……作为）to take something as, to take something for

【课文】人们把圆月当作团圆的象征，把中秋节作为亲人团聚的日子。

【例句】西方人把十三当作不吉利的数字，就像中国人把四作为不吉利的数字一样。

People in the West consider thirteen to be an inauspicious number just as Chinese people consider four to be inauspicious.

2. 眼看……却 soon (almost, in no time)...but

【课文】眼看织女就在面前，却被王母娘娘察觉了。

【例句】眼看英国队就要把足球踢进球门，却被意大利队的守门员一脚踢开了。

It seemed that the British team would kick the soccer ball into the goal in no time, but the Italian goalie kicked it aside.

3. 每……就 whenever

【课文】后来，每到七月初七，人们就会抬头仰望星空。

【例句】李太太每次经过大学医院就要对儿子说："你是在这个医院出生的。"

Whenever Mrs. Li passed by the university hospital, she would say to her son: "You were born in this hospital."

4. 在……帮助下 with the help of

【课文】在老黄牛的帮助下，他飞到了天上。

【例句】十年前，张先生在朋友的帮助下开了一家小餐馆，现在已经是一个全国连锁店的老板了。

Ten years ago, with the help of his friends, Mr. Zhang opened a small restaurant. Now he is already the owner of a national chain.

三、 成语 IDIOMS

1. 相亲相爱 to love each other

【课文】婚后，他们男耕女织，相亲相爱。

【例句】王先生和王太太结婚三十多年了，还像新婚夫妻一样相亲相爱。

Mr. Wang and his wife have already been married for over thirty years, but they still love each other like newlyweds.

2. 波涛汹涌 surging waves

【课文】她拔下头上的金钗，在牛郎与织女之间一划，立刻出现了一条波涛汹涌的银河。

【例句】大海是那么的神奇，有时候平静得像一面 镜子，有时候却波涛汹涌，把大船都打翻了。

The ocean is so mysterious. Sometimes it is smooth like a mirror, but other times it has surging waves, and even overturns large boats.

3. 热气腾腾 steaming hot

【课文】比如热气腾腾的火锅，说明红红火火。

【例句】小芳下班回家，看到妈妈为她做的一桌热气腾腾的饭菜，才想起今天是自己的生日。

Xiao Fang came home after work and saw a table laden with her mother's warm, steamy dishes, and realized that today was her birthday.

4. 辞旧迎新 to bid farewell to the old and usher in the new

【课文】吃了年夜饭，孩子们要到院子里去放爆竹，也叫放鞭炮，一直放到午夜以后，表示辞旧迎新。

【例句】每年除夕，成千上万的人在纽约的时报广场等着象征辞旧迎新的水晶球掉下来。

Every New Year's Eve, thousands of people wait in Times Square for the crystal ball to drop, which symbolizes a farewell to the old and ushering in the new.

5. 家家户户 every family, every household

【课文】除夕家家户户都一边吃年夜饭，一边看电视里的春节晚会的节目。

【例句】过感恩节的时候，家家户户都要吃一个大火鸡。

At Thanksgiving, each family will eat a big turkey.

练习 Exercises

一、 填名词

Fill in the blanks with appropriate nouns to form adjective-noun phrases.

1. 主要的 ＿＿＿＿ ＿＿＿＿
2. 重要的 ＿＿＿＿ ＿＿＿＿
3. 贫苦的 ＿＿＿＿ ＿＿＿＿
4. 美丽的 ＿＿＿＿ ＿＿＿＿
5. 忠厚的 ＿＿＿＿ ＿＿＿＿
6. 可爱的 ＿＿＿＿ ＿＿＿＿
7. 汹涌的 ＿＿＿＿ ＿＿＿＿
8. 忠贞的 ＿＿＿＿ ＿＿＿＿
9. 强大的 ＿＿＿＿ ＿＿＿＿
10. 痛苦的 ＿＿＿＿ ＿＿＿＿
11. 隆重的 ＿＿＿＿ ＿＿＿＿
12. 丰盛的 ＿＿＿ ＿＿＿＿
13. 吉祥的 ＿＿＿＿ ＿＿＿＿

二、 选词填空

Fill in the blanks using the words provided.

（当然、其他、原来、不料、据说、随着）

1. 他是我们学校的短跑冠军，＿＿＿＿＿＿他一百米能跑九秒八。

2. 他中文说得那么好，我一直以为他是中国人，现在才知道＿＿＿＿＿＿他是韩国人。

3. 大家都满心欢喜地等着他下午回来，＿＿＿＿＿＿他竟错过了那班车。

4. ＿＿＿＿＿＿天气渐渐变暖，人们经常在屋前屋后的花园里整理草木，邻居间讲话的机会就多了。

5. 这瓶桔子水一个星期前就过期了，你喝了＿＿＿＿＿＿会肚子痛了。

6. 昨天只有他一个人喝醉了，＿＿＿＿＿＿人都喝得不多。

三、用句型造句

Compose sentences using the sentence patterns below.

1. 把……当作，把……作为
2. 眼看……却
3. 每……就
4. 在……帮助下

四、用本课的成语改写句子

Rewrite each sentence using idioms you have learned in this lesson.

1. 今天特冷，可我们全家聚在一起，吃着很热的火锅，太温暖了！
2. 在喜宴上，大家举杯祝贺新郎新娘生活幸福，早生贵子。
3. 国庆节快到了，每家门前都插了一面国旗。
4. 最幸福的事就是每年都可以和家人一起欢度这迎接新年的时刻。
5. 在游船上，大家都跑来跑去玩儿，小林却喜欢看着不平静的大海，思考自己的未来。

五、选择题

Choose the correct word or phrase to complete each sentence.

1. 中国最主要的传统节日是 ________。
   a. 中秋节　　b. 端午节
   c. 春节　　　d. 清明节
2. 农历四、五、六三个月是 ________ 天。
   a. 春　　　　b. 夏
   c. 秋　　　　d. 冬
3. 中国的月亮女神是 ________。
   a. 织女　　　b. 嫦娥
   c. 白素贞　　d. 王母娘娘
4. 农历 ________ 是端午节。
   a. 正月初一　　b. 五月初五
   c. 七月初七　　d. 八月十五

5. 屈原是 _________ 国的大臣。
    a. 秦　　　　　　　b. 齐
    c. 楚　　　　　　　d. 赵
6. 端午节要吃 _________。
    a. 年糕　　　　　　b. 汤圆
    c. 月饼　　　　　　d. 粽子

六、改错

Correct the sentences below.

1. 端午节是仅次于春节的第二大传统节日。
2. 农历每月初一是圆月。
3. 七夕节是在晚秋。
4. 牛郎抱起两个孩子，去找织女。
5. 王母娘娘拔下头上的金钗，在牛郎与织女之间一划，立刻出现了一条波涛汹涌的牛奶河。
6. 很多人把中秋节作为中国的情人节。
7. 除夕夜，家家户户都一边吃年夜饭，一边上网拜年。

七、回答问题

Answer the questions below.

1. 中国有哪些重要节日？
2. 哪一天是中秋节？
3. 农历哪一天是圆月？
4. 中秋夜，家家户户在一起做什么？
5. 为什么王母娘娘要把织女抓回宫里？
6. 鹊桥是怎么搭起来的？
7. 银河边两颗较大的星是什么星？
8. 屈原怎么会被流放到边远地区？
9. 屈原在流放期间写的诗中，表达了什么感情？
10. 屈原为什么要自杀？
11. 赛龙舟的活动是怎么发展起来的？
12. 粽子的起源是什么？
13. 为什么年夜饭要吃鱼？

14. 为什么除夕晚上要放鞭炮？
15. 年初一吃年糕有什么象征意义？
16. 年初一吃汤圆有什么寓意？

八、英译中

Translate the passages below into Chinese.

1. The Lantern Festival falls on the fifteenth day of the first lunar month —
   usually February or March in the Western calendar. Lanterns of various shapes
   and sizes are hung in the streets, attracting countless visitors. Children will
   excitedly carry self-made or purchased lanterns to stroll with on the streets.

2. "Guessing lantern riddles" ① is an essential part of the festival. Lantern
   owners write riddles on pieces of paper and post them on lanterns. If visitors
   have solutions to the riddles, they can pull the papers out and go to the lantern
   owners to check their answers. If they are right, they will receive little gifts.

   【生词】① Guessing lantern riddles: 打灯谜 or 猜灯谜

3. In the daytime during the Lantern Festival, performances such as dragon
   lantern dances, lion dances, and land boat dances will be staged. At night, in
   addition to the magnificent lanterns, fireworks make a beautiful sight. Most
   families save some fireworks from the Spring Festival and set them off during
   the Lantern Festival. On the first full moon of the New Year, people really
   enjoy the fireworks and bright moon in the sky.

九、中译英

Translate the passages below into English.

1. 饺子是中国北方人普遍喜欢吃的一种面食，民间习俗在春节吃
   饺子。饺子宴，是以饺子为主的宴席，是1980年代在西安兴起
   的。有的饺子宴有108种饺子。有不同做法的饺子，如蒸饺、
   煮饺、煎饺、炸饺等。饺子的的馅儿也各有不同，如猪肉、鸡
   肉、鱼虾、蔬菜等。也有不同的口味，如咸、甜、酸、辣等。
   更有不同的形状，如形形色色的花果动物等。很多饺子的名称
   都富有诗情画意，如彩蝶飞舞、鱼跳龙门、群龙闹海、一路顺
   风等。一盘盘饺子赏心悦目、令人既食欲大开，又不忍动筷

子。所以有人说：不看秦始皇兵马俑，不算真到西安；不吃饺子宴，也不算真到西安。

2. "八月十五月儿圆，中秋月饼香又甜。"中秋吃月饼，和端午吃粽子、春节吃饺子一样，是中国民间的传统习俗。好的月饼皮薄馅大、色泽金黄、造型美观，图案花纹玲珑浮凸。馅心有豆沙、莲蓉、果仁、蛋黄、火腿等。古往今来，人们把月饼当作吉祥、团圆的象征。每逢中秋，皓月当空，合家团聚，品饼赏月，谈天说地，尽享天伦之乐。

十、故事复述

Retell the following stories:

1. 鹊桥相会
2. 屈原沉江

十一、作文

Write a short composition of approximately three hundred characters on one of the topics below.

【题目一】美丽的圣诞树

【提示】写一个圣诞节。你装点了圣诞树？写了贺卡？唱了哪些歌？收到什么礼物？吃了什么菜？圣诞夜和圣诞日都做了什么？

【题目二】响亮的爆竹声

【提示】写一个在中国过的春节：放爆竹、年夜饭、拜年、红包等等。中国的节日跟西方的节日有什么相同和不同的地方？

十二、成语故事

Describe the origins of the two idioms below.

1. 亡羊补牢
2. 望梅止渴

FOOD AND DRINK 饮食

Li Bai Gets Drunk and Wu Song Beats the Tiger
太白醉酒和武松打虎

中国地大物博、历史悠久，因此各地的菜肴都各有特色。比如，四川菜偏辣，上海菜较甜。但不管哪个地方的烹饪，都要求色、香、味俱佳。餐饮还要讲究情趣，所以菜单上常能看到"全家福"、"东坡肉"、甚至"龙凤呈祥"这样的菜名。

中国也生产各种好酒，像白酒中的茅台和啤酒中的青岛等。历代都有不少饮酒的故事。很多诗人觉得喝了酒，想像力会很丰富，会有写诗的灵感。

唐朝的大诗人李白被后人称为"诗仙"，可是他自称是"酒仙"。他的朋友杜甫说"李白一斗诗百篇。"李白写过一首题为《月下独酌》的诗，头四句是"花间一壶酒，独酌无相亲，举杯邀明月，对影成三人。"这首诗为后人所传诵，"举杯邀明月"也成了李白的经典形象。他有很多饮酒赋诗的故事，"太白醉酒"成为很多戏曲的题材。

跟文人一样，古代的武将也喜欢喝酒。他们觉得喝了酒以后会勇气倍增，武艺更高强。著名长篇小说《水浒传》中有一个叫武松的英雄就是在酒后徒手打死一只老虎的。

一次，武松回家探望哥哥，路过一座山，叫景阳冈。山下有一个酒店，门前挂着一面旗，写着五个字："三碗不过冈。"武松进店要了两斤熟牛肉，连喝了三大碗酒。武松一边叫好酒，一边要店主人再拿酒来。店主人说："你没看到那旗上写的吗？我的酒很厉害，喝了三碗就要醉了，过不了景阳冈。"但武松酒量特别大，竟一连喝了十八碗。

喝完酒要出门的时候，店主人说山上最近出现了一只大老虎，要武松等人多的时候一起上山。但武松不怕，提着根木棍，醉醺醺地走上山去。到了山顶后，忽然一阵狂风，一只大老虎朝武松扑了过来。武松急忙跳开，并趁猛虎转身的一霎间，举起木棍，朝虎头猛打下去。只听"喀嚓"一声，木棍打在树上，折成两段。老虎又向武松扑过来，武松扔掉半截棍，左手揪住老虎头上的皮，把它的头按到地上，右手提起铁锤般的拳头，不停地朝虎头打下去。没多久，就把老虎打得趴在地上动不了了。武松从此成了威名远扬的打虎英雄。

词汇一 VOCABULARY I

饮食	飲食	yǐnshí	food and drink, diet
菜肴	菜肴	càiyáo	(meat) dishes
偏		piān	to incline, to lean to one side
烹饪	烹飪	pēngrèn	cuisine, culinary arts
俱		jù	都
佳		jiā	好
情趣		qíngqù	delight and relish
龙凤呈祥	龍鳳呈祥	lóngfèng chéngxiáng	prosperity brought by the dragon and the phoenix, extremely good fortune
呈		chéng	to present
祥		xiáng	luck, auspiciousness
白酒		báijiǔ	liquor, spirits
灵感	靈感	línggǎn	inspiration
仙		xiān	celestial being, immortal
斗		dǒu	large container for wine
独	獨	dú	alone
酌		zhuó	to pour wine, to drink
壶	壺	hú	kettle, pot
题材	題材	tícái	subject, topic
武将	武將	wǔjiāng	military officer, general
勇气	勇氣	yǒngqì	courage
倍增	倍增	bèizēng	to double, to multiply
武艺	武藝	wǔyì	martial arts skills
高强		gāoqiáng	to excel at, to be a master of

英雄		yīngxióng	hero
徒手		túshǒu	barehanded, unarmed
探望		tànwàng	to pay a visit
面		miàn	measure word for flat and smooth objects such as flags and mirrors
旗		qí	flag
冈	岡	gāng	mountain ridge
斤		jīn	unit of weight (equal to half a kilogram)
熟		shú	cooked
酒量		jiǔliàng	capacity for drink
竟		jìng	unexpectedly, surprisingly
一连	一連	yīlián	successively, in a row
棍		gùn	rod
醉醺醺		zuìxūnxūn	drunkenly
顶	頂	dǐng	top, peak
阵	陣	zhèn	gust; measure word for wind, rain, etc.
扑	撲	pū	to pounce, to dash at
猛		měng	fierce, violent, powerful
一霎间	一霎間	yīshàjiān	in a wink, in a flash
喀嚓	喀嚓	kāchā	crack, snap (sound)
折		shé	to break, to snap
段		duàn	measure word for a section of something
扔掉		rēngdiào	to throw away
截		jié	measure word for a section of something
揪		jiū	to hold tight, to grab
皮		pí	skin
按		àn	to press, to push down
铁锤	鐵錘	tiěchuí	iron hammer
般		bān	sort, kind
拳头	拳頭	quántóu	fist
趴		pā	to lie prostrate
威名	威名	wēimíng	fame (won by military/martial exploits)
扬	揚	yáng	to spread, to make known

专名一 PROPER NAMES I

太白		Tàibái	Li Bai's style name
武松		Wǔ Sōng	hero from the novel *The Water Margin*
四川		Sìchuān	Sichuan Province
东坡	東坡	Dōngpō	Su Shi (also known as Su Dongpo, 1037–1101), Song poet, calligrapher, and statesman
茅台		Máotái	brand of liquor produced in the town of Maotai, Guizhou 贵州 Province
青岛	青島	Qīngdǎo	Qingdao City, in Shandong Province
杜甫		Dù Fǔ	Tang poet (712–770)
水浒传		Shuǐhǔ zhuàn	*The Water Margin*, one of the Four Great Classical Novels
景阳冈		Jǐngyáng gāng	mountain in Shandong Province

小故事 Ministory
Banquet at Hongmen 鸿门酒宴

设宴请客，气氛应该很友好，但也有例外。

秦朝末年，刘邦与项羽各自攻打秦朝的军队。刘邦兵力虽不及项羽，但先打破首都咸阳。项羽的大军也很快赶到了，驻扎在附近的鸿门。刘邦担心被项羽消灭，表示愿意谢罪。项羽就请刘邦来鸿门赴宴。

鸿门宴上，虽有不少美酒佳肴，气氛却非常紧张。项羽的军师范增，坚决主张杀掉刘邦。在酒宴上，他一再示意项羽发令，但项羽却犹豫不决。范增就叫将军项庄来舞剑，为酒宴助兴，趁机杀掉刘邦。刘邦的军师张良等人保护了刘邦，并帮助他逃了回去。

从此，鸿门宴就成了不怀好意的宴请的代名词。

词汇二 VOCABULARY II

设宴	設宴	shèyàn	to give a banquet
气氛	氣氛	qìfēn	atmosphere
例外		lìwài	exception

驻扎	駐紮	zhùzhā	(of troops) to be stationed
谢罪	謝罪	xièzuì	to offer an apology
坚决	堅決	jiānjué	firm, resolute
一再		yīzài	time and again
示意		shìyì	to signal, to hint
发令	發令	fālìng	to give an order
犹豫不决	猶豫不決	yóuyù bùjué	to hesitate, to remain undecided
舞剑	舞劍	wǔjiàn	to perform swordplay
助兴	助興	zhùxìng	to add to the fun, to liven things up
趁机	趁機	chènjī	to take the opportunity to do something
代名词	代名詞	dàimíngcí	another name, synonym

专名二 PROPER NAMES II

鸿门	鴻門	Hóngmén	name of an ancient place near present-day Xi'an 西安
咸阳	咸陽	Xiányáng	Qin capital, west of present-day Xi'an
范增	范增	Fàn Zēng	strategist of Xiang Yu's
项庄	項莊	Xiàng Zhuāng	general of Xiang Yu's
张良	張良	Zhāng Liáng	strategist of Liu Bang's

小知识 Knowledge
Gongbao Chicken 宫保鸡丁

　　宫保鸡丁是一道有名的四川菜，在海内外都很受欢迎。有些餐馆的菜单上写成了"宫爆鸡丁，"是因为有人认为烹饪的方法为"爆炒"。其实这是一种误解，没有弄清楚"宫保鸡丁"的来历。

　　这道菜的发明者丁宝桢是清朝的四川总督。丁宝桢对烹饪很有研究，爱吃鸡肉和花生米，尤其喜好辣味。他创制了一道将鲜嫩的鸡丁、香脆的花生，加上红辣椒，下锅爆炒而成的美味佳肴。客人吃了都赞不绝口。后来他被朝廷封为"太子少保"，人称"丁宫保"，这道菜就被称为"宫保鸡丁"。

词汇三 VOCABULARY III

鸡丁	雞丁	jīdīng	chicken cubes
丁		dīng	small cubes (of meat or vegetables)
海内外		hǎinèiwài	at home and abroad
爆炒		bàochǎo	to quickfry
误解	誤解	wùjiě	to misunderstand
来历	來歷	láilì	origin, background, past history
道		dào	measure word for dishes, etc.
发明者	發明者	fāmíngzhě	inventor
总督	總督	zǒngdū	governor general
花生米		huāshēngmǐ	shelled peanut, peanut kernel
创制	創制	chuàngzhì	to create
将		jiāng	把
鲜嫩	鮮嫩	xiānnèn	fresh and tender
脆		cuì	crisp, crunchy
辣椒		làjiāo	hot pepper
锅	鍋	guō	pot, pan
赞不绝口	讚不絕口	zànbù juékǒu	to praise unceasingly
朝廷		cháotíng	imperial court
封		fēng	to confer (a title, territory, etc.) upon, to appoint
太子少保		tàizǐ shàobǎo	junior guardian of the crown prince
太子		tàizǐ	crown prince

专名三 PROPER NAMES III

丁宝桢	丁寶楨	Dīng Bǎozhēn	Qing governor (1820–1886)

语言点 Language Points

一、词语 WORDS

1. 甚至 even

【课文】餐饮还要讲究情趣，所以菜单上常能看到"全家福"、"东坡肉"、甚至"龙凤呈祥"这样的菜名。

【例句】方先生是个好经理，可不是一个好爸爸，他甚至不去参加他女儿的钢琴独奏音乐会。

Mr. Fang is a good manager, but not a good father. He didn't even attend his daughter's solo piano concert.

2. 特别 especially, particularly

【课文】武松酒量特别大，竟一连喝了十八碗。

【例句】这家酒店特别注重服务态度，每一位员工在工作时都必须保持微笑。

This hotel especially emphasizes good service and manners. All staff members must smile at work.

3. 竟 unexpectedly, surprisingly

【课文】武松酒量特别大，竟一连喝了十八碗。

【例句】他去北京大学念过一个暑期班，就说自己是个"老北京，"可是竟把"涮羊肉"说成"刷羊肉"。

He took a summer class at Beijing University and always says that he is an "old Beijinger." But, surprisingly, he says "shua yangrou" for "shuan yangrou."

4. 只管 just, merely

【课文】右手提起铁锤般大小的拳头，尽平生之力，只管朝虎头打下去。

【例句】人家请你吃饭你怎么只管吃不说话呢？多没礼貌啊。

People invited you for a meal. How can you just eat without saying a word? How rude!

5. 趁机 to take the opportunity to do something

【课文】范增就叫将军项庄来舞剑，为酒宴助兴，趁机杀掉刘邦。

【例句】这次去加拿大旅游，趁机去看了一下多年不见的老朋友。

When we went to Canada, we took the opportunity to visit some old friends whom we had not seen for many years.

6. 尤其 especially, particularly

【课文】丁宝桢对烹饪很有研究，爱吃鸡肉和花生米，尤其喜好辣味。

【例句】这位教授虽然是美国人，但对中国古文字很有研究，尤其是甲骨文。

Although this professor is American, he does a lot of research on the ancient Chinese language, especially Shang dynasty oracle bone script.

二、 句型 SENTENCE PATTERNS

1. 不管 ...... 都 no matter, regardless of

【课文】不管哪个地方的烹饪，都要求色、香、味俱佳。

【例句】不管中国人美国人，到了他家，都要脱掉鞋子才能进屋。

Whether Chinese or American, when anyone enters his home, he needs to take off his shoes.

2. 像 ...... 等 such as

【课文】中国也生产各种好酒，像白酒中的茅台和啤酒中的青岛等。

【例句】他俩有着共同的兴趣爱好，像一边喝红酒一边听轻音乐等。

The two of them share common interests and hobbies, such as listening to light music while drinking red wine.

3. 跟 ...... 一样 the same as

【课文】跟文人一样，古代的武将也喜欢喝酒。

【例句】跟许多新移民的家长一样，小江的父母亲努力工作供他读书，希望他将来可以学有所成。

Like many parents who are new immigrants, Xiao Jiang's parents worked very hard to afford his education and hoped he could succeed through education.

4. V 不了 to be unable to do something

　　【课文】没多久，就把老虎打得趴在地上动不了了。

　　【例句】他每天晚上都会把第二天要做的事情写好，这样就忘
　　不了了。

　　Every night he writes down the things he needs to do the next day, so he
　　will not forget them.

5. V 成了 to become, to turn into

　　【课文】有些餐馆的菜单上写成了"宫爆鸡丁，"是因为有人
　　认为烹饪的方法为"爆炒"。

　　【例句】小英和她的姐姐长得像极了。今天在聚会上我把她姐
　　姐当成小英了。

　　Xiao Ying looks extremely similar to her sister. Today at the party I took
　　her sister to be Xiao Ying.

6. 对......有研究 having considerable knowledge of

　　【课文】丁宝桢对烹饪很有研究，爱吃鸡肉和花生米，尤其喜
　　好辣味。

　　【例句】她对饮食很有研究，吃什么东西都要先仔细阅读包装
　　上写的营养成分。

　　She is very knowledgeable about the culinary arts; whatever she eats, she
　　carefully reads the nutrition facts on the package first.

三、成语 IDIOMS

1. 地大物博 vast land and rich resources

　　【课文】中国地大物博、历史悠久，因此各地的菜肴都各有特
　　色。

　　【例句】这个国家地大物博，可是人口不多，所以很欢迎移
　　民。

　　This country has vast land and rich resources, but not a large population;
　　therefore, it welcomes immigrants.

2. 威名远扬 military or martial fame spread far and wide

　　【课文】武松从此成了威名远扬的打虎英雄。

　　【例句】打了这个大胜仗后，李将军威名远扬，敌人听到他的
　　名字就害怕。

　　After the big victory, General Li's fame spread far and wide; enemies grew
　　scared just hearing his name.

3. 犹豫不决 to hesitate, to remain undecided

【课文】在酒宴上，他一再示意项羽发令，但项羽却犹豫不决。

【例句】她的性格就是犹豫不决，连买个什么样的冰淇淋也要考虑半天。

It's her nature to hesitate—she will deliberate for a long time even as to what type of ice cream to buy.

4. 不怀好意 to have malicious intentions

【课文】从此，鸿门宴就成了不怀好意的宴请的代名词。

【例句】电梯里进来一位男子，不怀好意地看着身旁的女士。

A man entered the elevator and looked at the lady next to him with bad intent.

5. 赞不绝口 to praise unceasingly

【课文】客人吃了都赞不绝口。

【例句】雄伟壮丽的长城给游客留下了深刻的印象，大家都赞不绝口。

The magnificent Great Wall left a profound impression on the tourists. Everybody praised it unceasingly.

练习 Exercises

一、填名词

Fill in the blanks with appropriate nouns to form adjective-noun phrases.

1. 厉害的 ＿＿＿ ＿＿＿
2. 友好的 ＿＿＿ ＿＿＿
3. 坚决的 ＿＿＿ ＿＿＿
4. 犹豫的 ＿＿＿ ＿＿＿
5. 鲜嫩的 ＿＿＿ ＿＿＿
6. 香脆的 ＿＿＿ ＿＿＿

二、选词填空

Fill in the blanks using the words provided.

（甚至、特别、竟、只管、趁机、尤其）

1. 刚开始上课，火警练习的就铃声响了，大家 ________ 到教学大楼外面去聊天。
2. 他玩电脑游戏越来越上瘾了，________ 经常玩通宵。
3. 小林喜欢唱中国歌，________ 是各种不同风格的民歌。
4. 这一个月里，你 ________ 准备考试，别的事都不用管了。
5. 我们这个城市冬天总是非常冷，可是去年冬天 ________ 没下过一场雪。
6. 他的听觉 ________ 敏锐，连一个绣花针掉到地上的声音都听得清楚。

三、用句型造句

Compose sentences using the sentence patterns below.

1. 不管 …… 都
2. 像 …… 等
3. 跟 …… 一样
4. V 不了
5. V 成了
6. 对 …… 有研究

四、用本课的成语改写句子

Rewrite each sentence using idioms you have learned in this lesson.

1. 昨天我们正在湖上划船，忽然起了一阵大风，把我们的小船打翻了，我们都成了"落汤鸡。"
2. 四川省面积大、物产丰富，人口众多，是中国的一个大省。
3. 老李不是个好人，连笑的时候都会让人觉得他有坏心。
4. 黄太太特别会做菜，大家一边吃一边不断地称赞她做得好。
5. 小梅考上了北京大学，在我们县里人人都知道她的大名了。
6. 他从小的梦想就是去美国留学，可是看着父亲紧锁的眉头，他竟对着录取通知书决不定该不该去了。

五、选择题

Choose the correct word or phrase to complete each sentence.

1. _________ 菜较辣。
    a. 上海　　b. 广东
    c. 四川　　d. 北京
2. 茅台是一种 _________。
    a. 红酒　　b. 黄酒
    c. 白酒　　d. 啤酒
3. 武松酒量特别大，竟一连喝了 _________ 碗酒。
    a. 三　　　b. 十
    c. 八　　　d. 十八
4. 设宴请客，_________ 应该很友好。
    a. 气氛　　b. 环境
    c. 态度　　d. 情绪
5. 刘邦兵力虽不及项羽，但先打破首都 _________。
    a. 鸿门　　b. 咸阳
    c. 长安　　d. 西安
6. 项羽的军师 _________，坚决主张杀掉刘邦。
    a. 项庄　　b. 张良
    c. 范曾　　d. 诸葛亮
7. 宫 _________ 鸡丁是一道有名的四川菜，在海内外都很受欢迎。
    a. 爆　　　b. 宝
    c. 包　　　d. 保

六、改错

Correct the sentences below.

1. 很多诗人觉得喝了酒会勇气倍增。
2. 唐朝的大诗人李白被后人称为"酒仙"。
3. 武松是《三国演义》里的一个英雄。
4. 店主人说山上最近出现了一只大狮子。
5. 武松提着根铁棍，醉醺醺地走上山去。
6. 到了山脚下，忽听一阵狂风呼啸，一只大老虎朝武松扑了过来。
7. 只听"喀嚓"一声，木棍打在虎头上，折成两段。

8. 鸿门宴上，有不少美酒佳肴，气氛非常友好。
9. 范增叫项庄来舞剑，为酒宴助兴。

七、回答问题

Answer the questions below.
1. 为什么中国各地的菜肴都各有特色？
2. 中国的烹饪有什么要求？
3. 红烧狮子头是个什么菜？
4. 中国有些什么名酒？
5. 杜甫是怎么描写李白的？
6. 武松回家探望哥哥，路过一座什么山？
7. 酒店门口的旗子上写着什么字？
8. 刘邦为什么要去鸿门赴宴？
9. 宫保鸡丁这道菜是怎么做的？

八、英译中

Translate the following passages into Chinese.
1. Beijing duck 北京鸭 is a famous Beijing dish favored by people all over China and around the world. It is known for its thin, crispy skin, and is traditionally sliced in front of diners by the cook. For many foreign tourists in Beijing, attending a Beijing duck feast is as popular as climbing the Great Wall.
2. Dongpo pork is a famous Chinese dish that is said to have been created by Song poet Su Dongpo. Su Dongpo was once demoted and sent to Hangzhou to serve as its magistrate. He did many good things for the people, including dredging the West Lake and building a long dike on it. Because of this project, the West Lake's original beauty was restored.
3. The local people praised Su Dongpo for the feat and presented pork to him to express their gratitude. Su Dongpo received a large amount of pork. He cooked it following his own recipe, and sent cooked pork back to every household. After that, all families began to cook Dongpo pork. It has become a traditional Hangzhou dish.

九、中译英

Translate the passages below into English.

1. 翻译下面小吃的名称：馄饨、粽子、春卷、锅贴、小笼包、豆沙包、叉烧包、生煎馒头、葱油饼、萝卜丝饼、粢饭糕、糖年糕、八宝饭、酒酿园子、茶叶蛋、臭豆腐

2. 翻译下面带"吃"字的词语：吃惊、吃苦、吃力、吃香、吃亏、吃醋、吃喜酒、吃馆子、吃白食、吃豆腐、吃鸭蛋、吃小灶、吃干饭、吃老本、吃得开、吃不消、吃不准、吃败仗、吃官司、吃耳光、吃苦头、吃回扣、吃闭门羹、吃后悔药、吃大锅饭、吃开口饭

十、故事复述

Retell the following stories:

1. 武松打虎
2. 鸿门宴

十一、作文

Write a short composition of approximately three hundred characters on one of the topics below.

【题目一】我最喜欢的中餐馆

【提示】你平时喜欢去哪家中餐馆吃饭？为什么？是环境好？还是服务好？是菜好？还是菜便宜？哪些菜你最喜欢吃？能介绍一下吗？

【题目二】中餐馆的菜单

【提示】你去中餐馆拿一份菜单。选几个有特色的菜名，介绍一下这几个菜：里边有哪些东西？这个菜是怎么做成的？好吃不好吃？

十二、成语故事

Describe the origins of the two idioms below.
1. 削足适履
2. 邯郸学步

十三、背诵

Recite the following from memory:
李白《月下独酌》诗的头四句

ETIQUETTE 礼仪

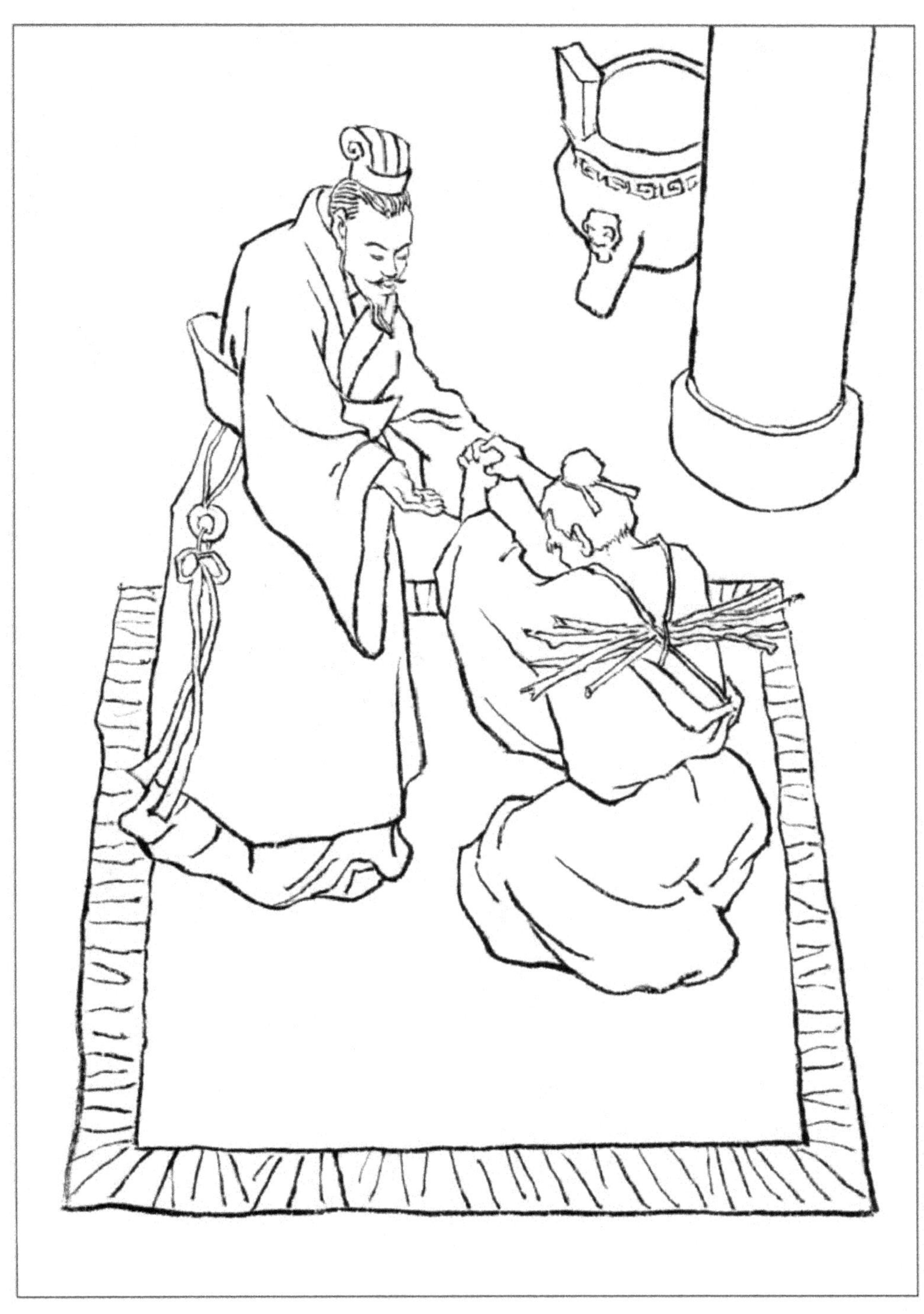

Standing in the Snow at the Teacher's Door and
Thrice Visiting the Thatched House
程门立雪与三顾茅庐

中国一向被称"礼仪之邦"，"礼"在传统社会无处不在。中国人的礼仪原则是谦恭待人、尊老敬贤。

尊敬老师是重要的传统礼仪美德。自古以来流传着许多这方面的故事。

宋朝的程颐是著名的儒家学者和教育家。他有个学生叫杨时，已经四十多岁了，学问相当好。一天，杨时来向程颐请教学问，正赶上老师在屋子里打盹儿。杨时恭恭敬敬地站在门口等候老师醒来。一会儿，天上下起鹅毛大雪，杨时却仍立在雪中。直到程颐一觉醒来，才发现站在门外的雪人。程颐深受感动，就更加悉心地教导杨时。后来，杨时也成了著名的儒家学者。

尊重人才既是礼仪，也是很多领导人成功的要诀。

汉朝末年，天下大乱，曹操、孙权和刘备各据一方。刘备听说隐居在山上的诸葛亮很有学识和才能，就和他的结拜兄弟关羽、张飞去请诸葛亮出山辅佐他。不巧，诸葛亮这天出去了，刘备只能失望地回去。不久，刘备又和关羽、张飞冒着大风雪第二次去请。不料诸葛亮又出外闲游去了。刘备只得留下一封信，表达自己对诸葛亮的仰慕之情。

过了一些时候，刘备准备再去请诸葛亮。关羽说诸葛亮也许是徒有虚名，未必有真才实学，不用去了。张飞却主张由他一个人去叫，如诸葛亮不来，就用绳子把他捆来。刘备把张飞责备了一顿，又和他俩第三次去请诸葛亮。这次，诸葛亮在家，可是正在睡午觉。刘备不敢惊动他，一直站着等到诸葛亮自己醒来，才一起坐下谈话。

诸葛亮见刘备有志替国家做事，而且态度这么诚恳，就答应刘备出山。后来，诸葛亮忠心耿耿地辅佐刘备，帮他建立了蜀国。"三顾茅庐"或"三请诸葛亮"也成为虚心求才的一段佳话。

词汇一 VOCABULARY I

礼仪	禮儀	lǐyí	ceremony and propriety, etiquette
顾	顧	gù	to pay a visit
茅庐	茅廬	máolú	thatched cottage
邦		bāng	nation, state, country
一向		yīxiàng	always, all along
原则		yuánzé	principle
谦恭	謙恭	qiāngōng	modest and respectful
待人		dàirén	to treat people (in a certain way), to conduct oneself toward others
贤	賢	xián	virtuous and capable, worthy
德		dé	virtue
方面		fāngmiàn	respect, aspect
儒家		rújiā	Confucian
学者	學者	xuézhě	scholar
学问	學問	xuéwèn	learning, knowledge, scholarship
相当	相當	xiāngdāng	quite, fairly, rather
赶上	趕上	gǎnshàng	to encounter, to come across, to run into (a situation), to be in time for
打盹儿	打盹兒	dǎdǔn	to doze off
等候		děnghòu	to wait
鹅毛	鵝毛	émáo	goose feather
悉心		xīxīn	wholehearted
教导	教導	jiàodǎo	to teach and guide
尊重		zūnzhòng	to respect
人才		réncái	talent, person of ability
要诀	要訣	yàojué	essential key to success
据	據	jù	to occupy, to hold

隐居	隱居	yǐnjū	to retire from public life and live in seclusion, to be a hermit
学识	學識	xuéshí	学问和知识
才能		cáinéng	ability, talent
结拜	結拜	jiébài	to become sworn brothers or sisters
辅佐	輔佐	fǔzuǒ	to assist (a ruler in governing a country)
不巧		bùqiǎo	unluckily
失望		shīwàng	to be disappointed
冒着	冒著	màozhe	to risk, to brave
闲游	閒遊	xiányóu	to stroll
仰慕		yǎngmù	to admire
徒有虚名		túyǒu xūmíng	with undeserved reputation, nominal, in name only
徒		tú	in vain, to no avail
未必		wèibì	not necessarily
由		yóu	by (somebody)
绳子	繩子	shéngzǐ	cord, rope, string
捆		kǔn	to tie
责备	責備	zébèi	to reproach, to blame
惊动	驚動	jīngdòng	to alarm, to startle
志		zhì	will, aspiration, ambition
替		tì	为
诚恳	誠懇	chéngkěn	sincere
忠心耿耿		zhōngxīn gěnggěng	loyal and devoted
虚心	虛心	xūxīn	open-minded, modest
求才	求才	qiúcái	to seek talent
佳话	佳話	jiāhuà	a story of a good deed

专名一 PROPER NAMES I

程颐	程頤	Chéng Yí	Neo-Confucian scholar (1033–1107)
杨时	楊時	Yáng Shí	Neo-Confucian scholar (1053–1135)
曹操		Cáo Cāo	king of Wei (r. 208–220)
孙权	孫權	Sūn Quán	king of Wu (r. 229–252)

刘备	劉備	Liú Bèi	king of Shu (r. 221–223)
关羽	關羽	Guān Yǔ	general of Liu Bei's (d. 220)
张飞	張飛	Zhāng Fēi	general of Liu Bei's (d. 221)

小故事 Ministory
A General's Apology 负荆请罪

战国时期，赵国有一个将军叫廉颇，一个大臣叫蔺相如。当初廉颇以军功升为大将军时，蔺相如还是个小官。后来，蔺相如出使强大的秦国，以机智和勇气维护了赵国的尊严和利益，因此被提升为宰相，地位比廉颇还要高。

廉颇生气了，他对人说："我有军功，而蔺相如就凭一张嘴，反而地位比我高。碰见蔺相如，我要羞辱他。"蔺相如听说以后，就处处忍让，尽量不和廉颇见面。有一次蔺相如乘车外出，看到廉颇远远过来，连忙吩咐车夫避开。

蔺相如身边的人都认为他胆小。蔺相如就跟他们解释说："你们想想，是秦王厉害呢，还是廉将军厉害？我敢在秦国的朝廷上当面斥责秦王，怎么会单单怕廉将军呢？秦国之所以不敢侵犯赵国，就是因为我们将相和睦。如果我和廉将军不和，秦国就有可乘之机了。"

廉颇听说了这些话，深感内疚。廉颇脱去上衣，背着荆杖，来到蔺相如家里请罪。于是，两人结成了生死与共的朋友。

词汇二 VOCABULARY II

负	負	fù	to carry on the back or shoulder
荆		jīng	bramble, thorn
请罪	請罪	qǐngzuì	to ask for punishment
当初	當初	dāngchū	at the beginning, originally
以		yǐ	because of
军功	軍功	jūngōng	military merits

升为	升為	shēngwéi	to be promoted to
机智	機智	jīzhì	wit, resourcefulness
维护	維護	wéihù	to safeguard, to preserve, to defend
尊严	尊嚴	zūnyán	dignity, integrity, honor
利益		lìyì	interest, benefit
提升		tíshēng	to promote
宰相		zǎixiàng	chief minister
凭	憑	píng	to rely on, to depend on
碰见	碰見	pèngjiàn	to meet unexpectedly, to run or bump into
羞辱		xiūrǔ	to humiliate
忍让	忍讓	rěnràng	to exercise forbearance
尽量	儘量	jǐnliàng	to the best of one's ability, as far as possible
吩咐		fēnfu	to tell, to instruct, to order
避开	避開	bìkāi	to avoid, to evade
胆小	膽小	dǎnxiǎo	timid, cowardly
解释	解釋	jiěshì	to explain
厉害	厲害	lìhài	formidable
敢		gǎn	to dare
当面	當面	dāngmiàn	face to face, to someone's face, in someone's presence
斥责	斥責	chìzé	to reproach, to reprimand
单单	單單	dāndān	only, alone
侵犯		qīnfàn	to invade
和睦		hémù	harmony, concord, amity
可乘之机	可乘之機	kěchéng zhījī	opportunity that can be exploited to someone's advantage
内疚		nèijiù	guilty conscience, compunction
脱		tuō	to take off, to undress
背		bēi	to carry on one's back
杖		zhàng	cane, stick
于是	於是	yúshì	therefore, as a result
生死与共	生死與共	shēngsǐ yǔgòng	together in life and death, through thick and thin

专名二 PROPER NAMES II

廉颇		Lián Pō	Zhao general (fl. 285-245 BCE)
蔺相如	藺相如	Lìn Xiàngrú	Zhao courtier (fl. 279-259 BCE)

小知识 Knowledge

The Four Books and Five Classics 四书五经

四书五经是四书和五经九部书的合称，是儒家的经典，古代学生的必读之书。

五经指《诗经》、《书经》、《易经》、《礼记》和《春秋》。《诗经》是中国最早的一部诗歌总集。《书经》是上古历史文件的汇编。《易经》说明宇宙阴阳变化。《礼记》记载和论述周朝的礼仪制度。《春秋》是鲁国的编年史。

四书指《论语》、《孟子》、《大学》和《中庸》四部书。《论语》记载孔子及其学生的言行。《孟子》记载孟子及其学生的言行。《大学》和《中庸》原是《礼记》中的两篇，南宋学者朱熹把它们拿出来单独成书，和《论语》、《孟子》合为四书。

词汇三 VOCABULARY III

合称	合稱	héchēng	common term, general term
指		zhǐ	to refer to
总集	總集	zǒngjí	anthology
上古		shànggǔ	ancient times, antiquity
文件		wénjiàn	documents
汇编	彙編	huìbiān	compilation, collection
宇宙		yǔzhòu	universe
阴阳	陰陽	yīnyáng	yin and yang, opposite forces in nature
记载	記載	jìzǎi	to put in writing, to record
论述	論述	lùnshù	to discuss, to explicate
编年史		biānniánshǐ	annals, chronicles
言行		yánxíng	words and deeds

专名三 PROPER NAMES III

鲁国	鲁國	Lǔguó	State of Lu
孟子	孟子	Mèngzǐ	Mencius (ca. 372–289 BCE), Confucian thinker and educator
南宋		Nán Sòng	Southern Song dynasty (1127–1276)
中庸		Zhōngyōng	*The Doctrine of the Mean*
朱熹		Zhū Xī	Confucian thinker and educator (1130–1200)

语言点 Language Points

一、词语 WORDS

1. 相当 quite, fairly, rather

【课文】他有个学生叫杨时，已经四十多岁了，学问相当好。

【例句】小高的中文相当好，甚至能说中文绕口令，比如"四十四只石狮子。"

Xiao Gao's Chinese is quite good; he can even do Chinese tongue twisters such as "sishisi zhi shishizi" (the forty-four stone lions).

2. 赶上 to encounter, to run into (a situation), to be in time for

【课文】一天，杨时来向程颐请教学问，正赶上老师在屋子里打盹儿。

【例句】他急忙奔出去就是为了能够赶上十点的车回家，参加女友的生日聚会。

He dashed out to catch the 10:00 bus back home so he could attend his girlfriend's birthday party.

3. 仍 still, yet, to remain the same as before

【课文】一会儿，天上下起鹅毛大雪，杨时却仍立在雪中。

【例句】虽然小强的爸爸妈妈想尽办法要引起他对中文的兴趣，包括带他去中国旅行，但他仍不想学中文。

Although Xiao Qiang's parents tried everything to raise his interest in Chinese—including taking him to China—he still does not want to study Chinese.

4. 也许 perhaps, probably

【课文】关羽说诸葛亮也许是徒有虚名，未必有真才实学，不用去了。

【例句】也许这条项链并不名贵，但因为是女儿送的，所以妈妈觉得那是无价之宝。

This necklace is probably not expensive; however, because it is a gift from her daughter, she feels it is a priceless treasure.

5. 未必 not necessarily

【课文】关羽说诸葛亮也许是徒有虚名，未必有真才实学，不用去了。

【例句】小刘总觉得世界上的事他都懂，可是事实上他说的未必都对。

Xiao Liu always feels that he knows everything in the world, but actually not everything he says is necessarily correct.

6. 凭 to rely on, to depend on

【课文】我有军功，而蔺相如就凭一张嘴，反而地位比我高。

【例句】凭着一口流利的中文，他在联合国找到了一个翻译的工作。

Because of his fluent Chinese, he got a job as a translator at the United Nations.

7. 反而 on the contrary, instead

【课文】我有军功，而蔺相如就凭一张嘴，反而地位比我高。

【例句】郑先生离开故乡三十多年了。在回乡的路上他一直很高兴，但在下飞机的时候他反而哭了。

Mr. Zheng left his hometown over thirty years ago. He was very cheerful all the way back, but after getting off of the airplane, he cried.

8. 处处 everywhere

【课文】蔺相如听说以后，便处处忍让，尽量不和廉颇见面。

【例句】春天到了，我们的校园里处处都可以闻到花香。

Spring is here. We can smell the fragrance of flowers everywhere on campus.

9. 尽量 to the best of one's ability, as far as possible

【课文】蔺相如听说以后，便处处忍让，尽量不和廉颇见面。

【例句】医生叫爸爸要尽量吃得清淡，所以妈妈做菜的时候油和盐都放得很少。

The doctor asked dad to eat as lightly as possible; therefore, mom always put as little oil and salt in her cooking as possible.

10. 于是 therefore, consequently

【课文】廉颇脱去上衣，背着荆杖，来到蔺相如家里请罪。于是，两人结成了生死与共的朋友。

【例句】听说跑步对减肥很有效，于是我决定每天六点钟起床去操场跑步。

It is said that jogging is very effective for weight loss; therefore, I've decided to get up at 6:00 every day and go jogging on the sports grounds.

二、 句型 SENTENCE PATTERNS

1. 既是……也是 to be both ... and ...

【课文】尊重人才既是礼仪，也是很多领导人成功的要诀。

【例句】小王既是学生会主席，也是大学的篮球队长，大家都喜欢他。

Xiao Wang is president of the Student Association and also captain of the college basketball team. Everybody likes him.

2. 不巧……只能 unluckily ... could only

【课文】不巧，诸葛亮这天出去了，刘备只能失望地回去。

【例句】小丽原来计划在花园里举行婚礼，不巧早上下起雨来，只能改在饭店里举行了。

Xiao Li originally planned to have her wedding in the garden. Unfortunately, it started to rain in the morning, so she could only change plans and hold the wedding in the restaurant.

3. 当初……后来 at the beginning ... later

【课文】当初廉颇以军功升为大将军时，蔺相如还是个小官。后来，蔺相如被提升为宰相，地位比廉颇还要高。

【例句】当初我们都以为他们会结婚，谁知，后来一个去了英国，一个去了中国，各奔东西。

At first we all thought they would get married. Who knew that later one would go to England and the other to China? Each pursued an individual course.

4. 是……还是 either . . . or

【课文】你们想想，是秦王厉害呢，还是廉将军厉害？

【例句】到底是读会计呢还是读文学呢？小王对专业的选择一直犹豫不决。

Should he study accounting or literature? Xiao Wang has always been hesitant to choose a major.

5. 之所以……是因为 because (with emphasis on the result)

【课文】秦国之所以不敢侵犯赵国，就是因为我们将相和睦。

【例句】我之所以选中文专业，是因为我觉得中国发展得很快，有很多机会。

The reason I have chosen a Chinese major is that I think China is developing very quickly and there will be many opportunities.

三、成语 IDIOMS

1. 徒有虚名 with undeserved reputation

【课文】关羽说诸葛亮也许是徒有虚名，未必有真才实学，不用去了。

【例句】那个大学名气很响，其实是徒有虚名。

That university is well known, but its reputation is undeserved.

2. 真才实学 real talent and genuine knowledge

【课文】关羽说诸葛亮也许是徒有虚名，未必有真才实学，不用去了。

【例句】孔教授是有真才实学的，大家都叫他"活词典。"

Professor Kong has real talent and genuine knowledge; everyone calls him a walking dictionary.

3. 可乘之机 opportunity that can be exploited to someone's advantage

【课文】如果我和廉将军不和，秦国就有可乘之机了。

【例句】爸妈去医院看外婆，小秋就有了可乘之机，开始大玩电脑游戏。

Dad and mom went to the hospital to visit grandma, so an opportunity arose for Xiao Qiu—he began playing many computer games.

4. 生死与共 together in life and death, through thick and thin

【课文】于是，两人结成了生死与共的朋友。

【例句】跟一个人结婚可是一件终身大事，一定要找一个能同甘共苦、生死与共的人。

Marriage is an important matter in life; you must find someone who can share the sweet and the bitter, and be with you through thick and thin.

练习 Exercises

一、填名词

Fill in the blanks with appropriate nouns to form adjective-noun phrases.

1. 谦恭的 ＿＿＿ ＿＿＿
2. 诚恳的 ＿＿＿ ＿＿＿
3. 机智的 ＿＿＿ ＿＿＿
4. 胆小的 ＿＿＿ ＿＿＿
5. 和睦的＿＿＿ ＿＿＿

二、选词填空

Fill in the blanks using the words provided.

(相当、赶上、仍、也许、未必、凭、反而、处处、尽量、于是)

1. 老吴来美国二十年，一直在中餐馆打工，到现在 ＿＿＿＿ 不会说英语。

2. 冬天下大雪的时候，我们 ＿＿＿＿ 不开车出门。

3. 本来说好今天回家的，但是公司请的新人还没来，＿＿＿＿ 我又要多工作几天了。

4. 小兰的数学 ＿＿＿＿ 好，你有做不出的题目，就去问她吧。

5. 我们开到纽约的时候，正 ＿＿＿＿ 下班的尖峰时刻，城里车堵得厉害。

6. 小程 ＿＿＿＿ 他的聪明和用功，进入了哈佛大学。

7. 小李从来不缺课，今天没来上课，＿＿＿＿ 是病了。

8. 他的话 ＿＿＿＿ 都对，你为什么总是相信他呢？

9. 老杨做股票想挣点钱，结果 ＿＿＿＿ 亏掉很多。

10. 父母 ＿＿＿＿ 为孩子着想，孩子长大了是不是也会这样对他们的父母呢？

三、用句型造句

Compose sentences using the sentence patterns below.

1. 既是 ......也是
2. 不巧 ......只能
3. 当初 ......后来
4. 是 ......还是
5. 之所以 ......是因为

四、用本课的成语改写句子

Rewrite each sentence using idioms you have learned in this lesson.

1. 那家饭馆的菜又贵又不好吃，名气虽然很大，实际上并不怎么好。
2. 经历了那么多风风雨雨后，他俩建立起了非常深厚的情谊。
3. 小偷挤上地铁后以为有了偷东西的机会，结果还是被抓住了。
4. 我选男朋友第一是看他有没有真正的学问，第二才看他长得帅不帅。

五、选择题

Choose the correct word or phrase to complete each sentence.

1. 自古以来 ________ 着许多尊师的故事。
   a. 流行　　b. 流传
   c. 流放　　d. 流动
2. 程颐深受感动，就更加 ________ 地教导杨时。
   a. 悉心　　b. 细心
   c. 关心　　d. 安心
3. 关羽说诸葛亮 ________ 是徒有虚名，未必有真才实学，不用去了。
   a. 或者　　b. 如果
   c. 不过　　d. 也许
4. 刘备把张飞责备了一 ________，又和他俩第三次去请诸葛亮。
   a. 次　　　b. 回
   c. 顿　　　d. 下

5.诸葛亮见刘备有志替国家做事，而且态度这么 ＿＿＿＿＿＿，就答
　应刘备出山。
　　　a. 诚心　　　　　b. 诚意
　　　c. 诚实　　　　　d. 诚恳
6.后来，蔺相如出使强大的秦国，以机智和勇气维护了赵国的
　＿＿＿＿＿＿ 和利益。
　　　a. 尊严　　　　　b. 尊贵
　　　c. 尊敬　　　　　d. 尊重
7.我敢在秦国的朝廷上当面 ＿＿＿＿＿＿ 秦王，怎么会单单怕廉将军
　呢？
　　　a. 责备　　　　　b. 斥责
　　　c. 侵犯　　　　　d. 进攻
8.秦国之所以不敢侵犯赵国，就是因为我们将相 ＿＿＿＿＿＿。
　　　a. 和平　　　　　b. 和睦
　　　c. 和气　　　　　d. 和美
9.于是，两人结成了 ＿＿＿＿＿＿ 的朋友。
　　　a. 忠心耿耿　　　b. 相亲相爱
　　　c. 威名远扬　　　d. 生死与共
10.《易经》说明 ＿＿＿＿＿＿ 阴阳变化。
　　　a. 世界　　　　　b. 地球
　　　c. 宇宙　　　　　d. 人间

六、改错

Correct the sentences below.

1. 程颐有个学生叫杨时，已经三十多岁了，学问相当好。

2. 一会儿，天上下起鸡毛大雪，杨时却仍立在雪中。

3. 尊重人才既是礼仪，也是很多领导人成功的秘密。

4. 刘备听说隐居在山上的诸葛亮很有学识和才能，就和他的结拜
　兄弟曹操、孙权去请诸葛亮出山辅佐他。

5. 不久，刘备又和关羽、张飞冒着大雨第二次去请。

6. 当初廉颇以军功升为大将军时，蔺相如已经是宰相了。

7. 蔺相如说："如果我和廉将军不和，秦国就没有可乘之机
　了。"

8. 四书指《论语》、《孟子》、《诗经》和《书经》四部书。

七、回答问题

Answer the questions below.

1. 中国人的礼仪原则是什么？
2. 一天，杨时来向程颐请教学问时，程颐正在做什么？
3. 刘备第三次去请诸葛亮的时候，诸葛亮正在做什么？
4. 为什么诸葛亮答应刘备出山？
5. 蔺相如怎么会被提升为宰相？
6. 蔺相如被提升为宰相后，廉颇为什么要生气？
7. 有一次蔺相如乘车外出，看到廉颇远远过来，他做了什么？
8. 为什么蔺相如对廉颇处处忍让？
9. 为什么廉颇要负荆请罪？
10. 五经是哪几部书？
11. 四书是哪几部书？
12. 《诗经》是部什么书？
13. 《论语》是部什么书？

八、英译中

Translate the passages below into Chinese.

1. Emperor Taizong of the Tang 唐太宗 (r. 626–649) is widely recognized as a wise ruler in Chinese history. He paid special attention to education and carefully selected teachers for the princes, such as Li Gang 李纲, Zhang Xuansu 张玄素, Wei Zheng 魏征, and Wang Gui 王圭, all men of great virtue who were highly esteemed.

2. On one occasion, Li Gang suffered a problem with his feet that made it impossible to walk. The imperial court had strict rules against officials riding in a carriage carried on men's shoulders. However, when Emperor Taizong learned about Li Gang's foot problems, he decreed that Li Gang be given the privilege of riding in a palanquin at court. He further ordered his prince to greet the teacher when he arrived at court.

3. On another occasion, Emperor Taizong learned that his fourth son, Li Tai 李泰, was not being respectful to his teacher, Wang Gui. He criticized his son in front of Wang Gui: "Next time you see your teacher, you must be as respectful to him as you are to me. Even the slightest digression is not allowed." From then on, Li Tai was courteous and respectful toward his teacher. His schoolwork also improved. Emperor Taizong's strict family rules called for all of the princes to respect their teachers and to value the teachings they received.

九、中译英

Translate the passages below into English.

1. 《孔融让梨》
   汉朝末年的孔融是孔子的后代。孔融四岁的时候，父亲带回一些梨给他们弟兄吃。因孔融最小，全家人都让他先挑。孔融拿了一个最小的梨。大家都很奇怪，父亲问他为什么要拣最小的拿，他回答说："我年龄最小，应当吃最小的梨。"从此，幼年孔融这种谦让的美德，受到人们的称赞。
2. 《六尺巷》
   清朝时安徽桐城有姓张和姓叶的两家邻居。张家有个儿子张英在京城做宰相，叶家也有个儿子在朝中当大官。这年两家都要造房子，为争地皮发生纠纷。张老夫人为此给儿子张英写信，要他帮忙。张英劝导老母亲，他往家里寄了一首诗："千里家书只为墙，再让三尺又何妨? 万里长城今犹在，不见当年秦始皇。"张家收到信，立即将院墙退后三尺。叶家见了，也很快把院墙让后三尺。中间空出的六尺巷道，被当地人称为"六尺巷"。两家互相谦让，被传为佳话。

十、故事复述

Retell the following stories:

1. 程门立雪
2. 三顾茅庐
3. 负荆请罪

十一、作文

Write a short composition of approximately three hundred characters on the topic below.

【题目】我的老师
【提示】写一位你的老师，从小学到大学都可以。他（她）的外貌和性格有什么特点？给你帮助最大的是什么？写一、两件给你印象最深刻的事。

十二、专题研究

Research the following topic online and report to the class.
简单介绍一下《论语》

ENGLISH TRANSLATIONS OF THE TEXTS 课文英译

LESSON 1 第一课
Calligraphy

"PREFACE TO THE *ORCHID PAVILION*" AND
"THE PAGODA OF MANY TREASURES"
《兰亭序》与《多宝塔》

The art of writing Chinese characters has enjoyed a long history. The art has existed for over 3,500 years—beginning with the oracle bone script of the Shang dynasty. Bronze inscription was used in the Zhou dynasty, seal script was used in the Qin dynasty, and clerical script was used in the Han dynasty. At the start of the Jin dynasty the formal script, cursive script, and running script had all been formed. What we now write is basically formal script. In calligraphic works, we can often find clerical script, cursive script, and running script. When people carve seals, seal script is still often used.

There were many outstanding calligraphers in Chinese history. Wang Xizhi of the Jin dynasty has been called the Sage of Calligraphy by later generations. He practiced calligraphy very diligently when he was young. There was a pond next to his house where he often washed his writing brushes and inkstones. After a long time, the water in the pond turned black. That pond became the famous "Ink Pond."

The most famous calligraphic work by Wang Xizhi is the "Preface to the *Orchid Pavilion*." Once, Wang Xizhi and his friends held a gathering in Lanting, Zhejiang, drinking wine and writing poems. Wang Xizhi wrote the "Preface to the *Orchid Pavilion*" on the spot. This work of calligraphy is refreshing and natural, like floating clouds and flowing water. The character *zhi* 之 appears more than twenty times in the piece, and surprisingly, none is similar to any other. Wang Xizhi later rewrote the "Preface to the *Orchid Pavilion*" many times, but none was as good as the original work. He thus took this piece of calligraphy to be a family heirloom. "Preface to the *Orchid Pavilion*" was regarded by later generations as the "Number One Running Script in the World."

About four hundred years after Wang Xizhi's death, Yan Zhenqing of the Tang dynasty again founded a new era of calligraphic art. His father passed away when he was three years old. His family was so poor that could not even afford to buy paper and writing brushes. Yan Zhenqing could only dip a broom in yellow slop and practice writing with it on the wall. He wrote a poem titled "An Exhortation to Study," which reads, "Lights at midnight and rooster's crow at dawn / Exactly the times for a man to study. / Black hairs know not to learn early, / White heads regret that it is too late to crack the books." Does this not describe his own diligent studies?

At that time during the Tang dynasty there were many rebellions. Yan Zhenqing bravely fought against the rebels. At age seventy-five, Yan Zhenqing went to the camp of a rebellious army to persuade them to surrender. When he arrived, over one thousand rebellious soldiers surrounded him, drawing their swords and pointing them at him. However, Yan Zhenqing kept his composure. Later, for a long time, Yan Zhengqing neither took the bait of the rebels nor succumbed to their threats. As a result, the rebels killed him.

People later said that Yan Zhenqing's character, which was "as bright as sun and moon, and as firm as metal and rock," fostered his calligraphic art. Each character in Yan Zhenqing's formal script is solid and strong. His representative works are "Pagoda of Many Treasures" and others. There is a Chinese saying that "script is like the person," and this is best exhibited by Yan Zhenqing.

EIGHTEEN VATS OF WATER 十八缸水

Wang Xianzhi was the seventh son of Wang Xizhi and studied calligraphy with his father from an early age. Once when the young Xianzhi was concentrating on practicing calligraphy, Wang Xizhi sneaked up behind him and suddenly extended his hand to take the writing brush from Xianzhi's hand. Xianzhi held the brush very firmly and thus did not lose it. The father was very happy and said, "This child will have a bright future."

One day, young Xianzhi asked his father, "Will I be good after three more years of practice?" Father shook his head. "Will five years do it?" Father shook his head again. Xianzhi got anxious: "Then would you let me know how many years are needed after all?" "Remember, you can write well only if you use up those eighteen vats of water in the yard."

Xianzhi practiced hard for another five years. He presented his father with a big pile of his calligraphy in hopes of hearing a few words of praise. To his surprise, Wang Xizhi shook his head while looking it over. When he saw the character *da* 大, he nodded, and offhandedly added one dot at the bottom to make *tai* 太.

Xianzhi then carried all of his writing to his mother and said, "I practiced another five years; furthermore, I strictly followed father's writing. Please take a careful look: what differences are still there between my writing and his?" Mother looked them over carefully for three days. Then, pointing to the dot that Wang Xizhi added to the character *da* 大, she said with a sigh, "My son used up three vats of water; only this dot looks like Xizhi's."

Xianzhi was greatly inspired by the words so he continued to practice painstakingly. Finally, he used up the eighteen vats of water. No pain, no gain. Wang Xianzhi also became a great calligrapher. He enjoyed the same fame as Wang Xizhi, and together they were called the "Two Wangs."

MAJOR DYNASTIES 主要朝代

There were many major and minor dynasties in Chinese history. Among them, there are ten important dynasties:

Zhou dynasty, 1046–256 BCE
Qin dynasty, 221–206 BCE
Han dynasty, 202 BCE–220 CE
Six Dynasties, 221–589
Sui dynasty, 581–617
Tang dynasty, 618–907
Song dynasty, 960–1279
Yuan dynasty, 1271–1368
Ming dynasty, 1368–1644
Qing dynasty, 1644–1911

The Zhou dynasty, which lasted nearly eight hundred years, was the longest. The Qin dynasty and Sui dynasty were both short, but both unified China and established important systems. The Han dynasty exerted a lasting influence upon China, which can be seen in phrases such as "Han people" and "Han language." The Six Dynasties is a collective term for six dynasties. Tang, Song, Yuan, Ming, and Qing are the last five major dynasties and are often mentioned together.

LESSON 2 第二课

Chinese Painting

"INK PLUM BLOSSOMS" AND "INK BAMBOO"
《墨梅图》 与 《墨竹图》

Traditional Chinese painting is called *guohua* (national painting) in its contracted form. It can be categorized into mountain-and-water paintings, flower-and-bird paintings, figure paintings, and other types. Chinese painting requires a perfect combination of poetry, calligraphy, and painting; therefore, many painters are poets and calligraphers as well. In addition, artists attach importance to the symbolic meanings of the animals and plants they paint. For example, they like to paint pine trees because Confucius said, "Only when the year turns cold do we realize that the pine and cypress are the last to fade." Similarly, bamboo is green during all four seasons and plum blossoms do not wither in severe cold, so artists often paint pine trees, bamboo, and plum blossoms together, calling them the "Three Friends in Cold Weather."

When discussing plum blossom paintings, one thinks of Wang Mian. A famous artist and poet of the Yuan dynasty, Wang Mian was born into a poor family. When he was young he read books while he herded buffalo. One day, he left his buffalo in the pasture and went by himself to a nearby school to listen to student recitations. When he came back at dusk he could not find his buffalo. As a result, he received a good thrashing from his father.

After he had grown up, Wang Mian did not have a career as a government official, but made a living by selling his paintings. He planted over one thousand plum trees in his yard and called himself "Master of the House of Plum Blossoms." He inscribed a poem on his painting titled "Ink Plum Blossoms": "On the tree next to the inkstone washing pond at my home, / Each flower blossoms as if painted in light ink. / They do not invite people to praise their fine colors, / Wanting only to keep the fresh spirit that fills the universe." The first and second lines describe the plum blossoms. The third and fourth lines praise the plum blossoms' character: they do not think to attract people with bright colors, but only to distribute fresh fragrance and letting it remain in the world. These two lines are also the poet's description of himself.

Bamboo, which also belongs to the "Three Friends in Cold Weather," also is a favorite of artists. Zheng Xie, styled Banqiao, of the Qing dynasty, was well known as a painter of bamboo. People often used the phrase "having painted bamboo in his mind" to describe the superior skill he had in bamboo painting. One day, Zheng Banqiao was sick in bed. He saw bamboo outside his window standing firm in a severe storm. He got up immediately and painted a piece called "Ink Bamboo." He inscribed a poem on the painting: "Biting into the green mountain and never letting go, / Roots are originally put down in the broken rocks. / It is still strong after much wear and tear, / No matter whether the wind blows from the east, west, south, or north." This poem illustrates the bamboo's environment and praises its spirit as well. Together, the poem and painting became a treasure passed down through the generations.

THE POET AND THE THIEF 赋诗送贼

Lying in bed in the dead of night, Zheng Banqiao suddenly saw a human figure through his paper windows. He thought, "This is bad—a thief has come. I am not strong enough to fight him, nor can I let him steal my things. What should I do?" After a little thinking, he recited in a soft voice, "Fine rain drizzling deep in the night, / A thief has entered my gate."

At this time the thief had already come into the house and was startled upon hearing this. He then heard, "A thousand volumes of poems and books are in my belly, / Not a half coin of gold or silver in my bed." The thief thought, "It turns out he is a poor man, so I will not steal from him." He turned and went out the door and heard the voice inside say, "Don't scare the dog with the yellow tail outside." The thief thought, "Since there is a dog, I must go over the wall to get out of here." Right before climbing the wall, he heard again, "Don't damage the orchid pot while you go over the wall." The thief took a look, and there was in fact a pot of orchids on the wall. At that time, the yellow dog ran to the thief and held him by biting him. Zheng Banqiao came out and recited two more lines, "I did not have time to put on my coat to see you off in this cold weather, / Raise your aspirations and turn over a new leaf."

FOUR TREASURES OF THE STUDY 文房四宝

Wenfang refers to the study of ancient literary men. Four Treasures of the Study is the collective name for *bi* (writing brush), *mo* (ink stick), *zhi* (paper), and *yan* (inkstone)—the four supplies used in writing and painting. Ancient Chinese literary men could not do without these four treasures.

Bi refers to the writing brush. Because calligraphy is categorized into small, medium, and large script, the brushes can also be designated small, medium, and large script brushes.

Mo is also quite an art. When writing, the ink should be ground thickly and evenly.

Zhi is one of the Four Great Inventions of ancient China. The Chinese started to make paper as early as in the Han dynasty. There is a kind of paper called *Xuan* paper, which is best for calligraphy and painting.

Yan is also called *yantai*. Some inkstones are made of very good stone selected especially for this purpose. They also feature exquisite carving; therefore, they are works of art themselves.

Of course, the Four Treasures of the Study are very important for calligraphers and painters. However, Yan Zhenqing's spirit in writing with a broom and yellow slop on the wall cannot be forgotten, either.

LESSON 3 第三课
Tang Poetry

"A NIGHT MOORING AT THE MAPLE BRIDGE" AND
"AN OCCASIONAL POEM UPON RETURNING TO MY HOMETOWN"
《枫桥夜泊》与《回乡偶书》

The Tang dynasty is the golden age of Chinese poetry. Even up to now, many parents still teach their children to recite Tang poems by memory. Young children have good memories; they can remember poems by reading them a few times and it often happens that they do not forget them their entire lives.

The first poem many children memorize is Li Bai's "Thoughts on a Still Night": "Bright moonlight in front of my bed, / I suspect it was frost on the ground. / Lifting my head, I watch the bright moon, / Lowering my head, I miss my hometown." Many children recite this poem by memory, possibly because it is quite short and the wording is very simple. But more important is that this poem vividly depicts the poet's homesickness while traveling.

Let us introduce two more poems. One is Zhang Ji's "A Night Mooring at the Maple Bridge": "The moon sets, crows cry, frost fills the sky, / Maple trees by the river, fishing lights, face a worried person abed. / From the Cold Mountain Temple outside Suzhou City, / The tolling of the midnight bell reaches the traveler's boat."

The Cold Mountain Temple, with a history of over 1,500 years, is west of the City of Suzhou. The first two lines of the poem present six images: the setting moon, crying crows, a sky full of frost, maple trees by a river, fishing lights, and a sorrowful person in bed. The first five are environmental, and the sixth is the subject. A frosty sky means deep autumn, and the setting moon means late night. The poet in the cabin, watching the maple trees and fishing lights and listening to the crow crying, could not fall asleep. In this situation, listening to the Cold Mountain Temple bell from afar, what kind of feelings would he have?

The other poem is He Zhizhang's "An Occasional Poem upon Returning to My Hometown": "I left my home in youth and now I return old, / The village accent hasn't changed, but my sideburns have grown gray. / Children see me but do not recognize me, / They ask with a smile, 'Hey, visitor, where are you from?'" He Zhizhang resigned his official post when he was eighty-six years old and returned to his hometown in Zhejiang. This poem is a narrative with a warm tone. However, read carefully, the poem is full of contrasts. "I left my home in youth" and "I return old" in the first line form a contrast of time. In fact, more than fifty years separated these two milestones in his life path. "The village accent hasn't changed" and "my sideburns have grown gray" in the second line form another pair of contrasts, describing the change (age) and no change (accent) that time has caused.

"Children see me" contrasts with "don't recognize me" in the third line, which describes the length of his absence from his hometown. The last line is children's words, very interesting, yet they also contain a pair of contrasts—that between the native and the visitor: he was supposed to be a native, but now has become a visitor. These four pairs of contrasts, going deeper level by level, describe the sadness of his leaving home for half a century, but also express the joy of "falling leaves returning to their roots."

TO PUSH OR TO KNOCK 推敲苦吟

Tuiqiao (pushing and knocking) is a frequently used word that is a metaphor for careful deliberation in writing or doing something. But why is it called pushing and knocking? There is a story behind it.

Once upon a time, Tang poet Jia Dao went to Chang'an to take exams. He rode a donkey on the street and thought about poetic lines. He thought of two good lines and recited them from the donkey's back: "Birds rested on the tree at the edge of the pond, / A monk pushed the door under the moon."

He liked those two lines but also intended to change the word "pushing" to "knocking." Not being able to decide quickly, he used his hands to make the gestures of pushing and knocking. He wasn't watching out, and his donkey rushed into an official's convoy. Only then did Jia Dao come to his senses. Coincidentally, this official was the great poet Han Yu. Hearing Jia Dao's explanations, Han Yu laughed heartily. He said to Jia Dao, "I would think 'knocking' is better. When visiting someone in the evening, 'knocking' is still more polite. Also, knocking in the deep silent night would make a little noise. Wouldn't that be interesting?" Jia Dao nodded continuously as he listened, and they became good friends from then on.

THE TOLLING BELL AT HANSHAN TEMPLE 寒山钟声

Since Zhang Ji wrote the poem "A Night Mooring at the Maple Bridge," the tolling of the Hanshan Temple bell has become very famous. Suzhou City started the event of "Listening to the Hanshan Bell on New Year's Eve" in 1979, which became a tradition; there are a few thousand participants every year. The Hanshan bell starts to strike at 23:42:10 on New Year's Eve, and rings every ten seconds. By midnight on New Year's Day, it rings 108 times altogether. These 108 rings imply two levels of leaving behind the old and welcoming the new. The first is that there are 12 months, 24 seasonal divisions, and 72 five-day units in the Chinese lunar calendar, adding up to exactly 108. Upon hearing the bell toll, we consider one year to have passed. Second, in Buddhism it is thought that there are many worries in human lives—108 altogether. Having heard the bell, one can be released from these worries and be safe and sound in the New Year. Since there is such a good deal, would you also like go to Hanshan Temple to listen to the bell?

LESSON 4 第四课

Chinese Instrumental Music

"THE HIGH MOUNTAIN AND FLOWING WATER" AND
"AMBUSH FROM ALL SIDES" 《高山流水》与《十面埋伏》

Traditional Chinese music is also called national music, *minyue* in its contracted form. *Minyue* includes many unique instruments and classic songs.

Qin is also called *guqin,* and is the oldest plucked instrument. It is said to have a history of over five thousand years. The *qin* piece "The High Mountain and Flowing Water" tells a touching story.

There was a famous *qin* player named Boya. One day, Boya was playing the *qin* on a mountain and a woodcutter named Zhong Ziqi listened on the mountainside for a long time. Ziqi told Boya that he heard music depicting the high Mount Tai and rushing Yellow River. Boya said excitedly: "What I played is the ancient song 'The High Mountain and Flowing Water.' You are really my *zhiyin* (person who knows music)!"

They agreed to meet at the same time and place the following year. The next year, Boya came to the mountain but did not see Ziqi. It turned out that Ziqi had passed away. Boya went to Ziqi's tomb and began playing "The High Mountain and Flowing Water" sadly. After he finished the song, he gave a long sigh, and threw his favorite *qin* onto a gray rock and broke it to pieces. He said, "My *zhiyin* is no longer in this world; for whom I can play this *qin?*" Later, people built a *qin* terrace at the place they met. Even now, people still use the word *zhiyin* to describe good friends who understand each other.

Unlike the graceful "The High Mountain and Flowing Water," the melody of the *pipa* piece "Ambush from All Sides" is quite exciting. "Ambush from All Sides" depicts the famous historical battle between Chu and Han. During the last years of the Qin, there were peasant uprisings in many places. The two strongest armies were the Han army led by Liu Bang and the Chu army led by Xiang Yu. In 202 BCE, Liu Bang's three hundred thousand troops encircled and destroyed Xiang Yu's one hundred thousand troops. After the war, Liu Bang established the Han dynasty.

This piece extensively uses the exquisite *pipa* technique to reproduce fiercely intense scenes of war. It seems that the audience can hear war drums, military bugles, shouts, and the sounds of horses galloping and weapons striking. No wonder people say that a *pipa* solo is comparable to the playing of a symphony orchestra.

BUTTERFLIES AMONG THE FLOWERS 花间彩蝶

Have you heard the violin concerto "Liang Zhu"? Do you know this love story?

In ancient times there was a beautiful girl named Zhu Yingtai who loved learning. She wholeheartedly wanted to go to Hangzhou to study. At that time girls could not attend school, so she disguised herself as a man and hit the road.

At school Yingtai and her classmate Liang Shanbo became good friends. Over the course of three years' studying together, Yingtai fell in love with Shanbo. However, all the while Shanbo did not know that Yingtai was a girl.

Yingtai's father missed his daughter and urged her to return home. Liang Shanbo, reluctant to part with her, accompanied her for eighteen miles on the way back home. When they parted, Yingtai told Shanbo that she had a sister at home, and asked Shanbo to come to her home to propose marriage. After a period of time, Shanbo came to the Zhu home. Only then did he find out that Yingtai was a girl. However, Yingtai's father had already promised a high official that Yingtai would marry his son. Shanbo was very sad to know this and soon died of illness.

Before Yingtai was forced to marry, she came to Shanbo's tomb. Her sorrow moved heaven and earth; in the fierce storm, Shanbo's tomb split and Yingtai jumped in. After a while, the storm ended and a colorful rainbow hung in the sky. Liang and Zhu transformed into butterflies and danced among hundreds of flowers.

This story was later adopted for Yue opera. At the end of the opera, all performers sing in unison: "The colorful rainbow is ten thousand miles long and hundreds of flowers bloom, / Butterflies among the flowers are paired. / Not to be separated for thousands of years and ten thousand generations, / They are Liang Shanbo and Zhu Yingtai."

ERHU AND SUONA 二胡唢呐

We have talked about two traditional Chinese music instruments: *guqin* and *pipa*. Now we will introduce two more.

Erhu is one of the major stringed instruments in traditional music. Its function is somewhat like that of the violin in the Western orchestra. Because the instrument has two strings, it is called *erhu*. Famous *erhu* solo pieces include "The Moon's Reflection in the Two Streams" and others.

Suona, also called *laba*, is a wind instrument used widely in folk ceremonies. In olden times, many celebrations would not do without *suona*, such as the sending of the dowry, following the bridal palanquin, holding a wedding banquet, making merry in the bridal chamber, and the bride's return to her parents' home. The famous *suona* song "Hundred Birds Revering the Phoenix" depicts the vigor of nature using lively melodies and the songs of hundred birds.

LESSON 5 第五课
Beijing Opera

THE WHITE SNAKE AND THE EMPTY CITY STRATAGEM
《白蛇传》 与 《空城计》

Beijing opera is a comprehensive art using many artistic forms—including drama, singing, instruments, dancing, martial arts, and makeup. The makeup of Beijing opera has distinctive features. Some male roles having peculiar characters or appearance use a facial design called "patterned face." Red face painting symbolizes loyalty; black, valor; yellow, ferocity; blue and green, hot temper; and white, craft and deceit.

Many Beijing operas have been adapted from historical stories or folk tales. *The White Snake* is indeed a famous folktale. The story begins in Song dynasty Hangzhou. A young man named Xu Xian met the White Lady, transformed from a white snake, and Little Green, transformed from a green snake, on the beautiful West Lake. Xu Xian and the White Lady fell in love and were married. They moved to Zhenjiang after their wedding, opened an herbal medicine shop, and lived happily. However, Fahai, a Buddhist monk of the Golden Mountain Monastery in Zhenjiang, did everything possible to break up Xu Xian and the White Lady. He used his supernatural powers to draw the White Lady into his alms bowl and pressed the bowl under the Leifeng Pagoda on the shore of the West Lake. Later, Little Green defeated Fahai, pushed over the Leifeng Pagoda, and rescued the White Lady.

More historical stories have been adapted for Beijing opera. *The Empty City Stratagem* tells the story of Zhuge Liang, from the historical novel *Romance of the Three Kingdoms*. During the last years of the Han dynasty, China was divided into the three kingdoms of Wei, Shu, and Wu. Zhuge Liang of Shu was an outstanding strategist. Once, Sima Yi, a general of Wei, brought an army of 150,000 to attack the West City, where Zhuge Liang was. At the time, Zhuge Liang had only 2,500 soldiers with him. Everyone went pale with fear when they heard the news of Sima Yi's approaching army.

Zhuge Liang gave orders unhurriedly. He asked the soldiers to open the city gates, and sent only a few soldiers disguised as civilians to sweep the roads in front of the gates. Zhuge Liang himself, in a robe and carrying a zither, went to the gate tower, sat down, and began to play the zither leisurely. When Sima Yi arrived at the city gates, he took a look, was quite confused, and ordered retreat. His assistant asked, "Is it possible that Zhuge Liang actually does not have troops?" Sima Yi said, "Zhuge Liang has always been prudent. Since the city gates are wide open, there must be an ambush laid inside. Let's retreat immediately!" After Sima Yi's withdrawal, Zhuge Liang heaved a sigh of relief, and wiped away the cold sweat on his forehead.

A BEIJING OPERA MASTER IN AMERICA 大师访美

Mei Lanfang was a Beijing opera master in modern China. In 1930, Mei Lanfang led his troupe to the United States to perform. In half a year, they had seventy-two shows in New York, Chicago, San Francisco, Los Angeles, Washington DC, Seattle, and other cities, and achieved great success. America was in the Depression at that time, but $6 tickets surprisingly sold for up to $40 in New York. After the curtain call for his last show in New York, Mei Lanfang stood in the front of the stage and shook hands with people from the audience. He shook hands for several dozen minutes but was still not done. It turned out that many people returned to the line after shaking hands with him.

During his visit to the United States, Mei Lanfang was conferred a doctorate by the University of Southern California. He made good friends with Charlie Chaplin and other artists. However, there was one particular American who did not have the chance to enjoy his performance: President Hoover. When Mei Lanfang performed in Washington DC, Hoover was out of town. Later Hoover made a special phone call to Mei Lanfang and invited him to perform in Washington DC again. However, due to his schedule, he was not able to make it. Both Mei Lanfang and Hoover felt this was regrettable.

CHINESE LOCAL OPERAS 地方戏曲

There are altogether more than three hundred local operas in China. Many local operas are named after their locations. For example, Beijing opera was developed in the Beijing area. Yue opera originated in the Shaoxing area, in Zhejiang Province, which was the State of Yue in ancient times. It is a major opera form that is second only to Beijing opera. Representative works include *Dream of the Red Chamber* and *The Butterfly Lovers*. Besides these, Hu opera is the local opera of Shanghai because Shanghai's alternate name is Hu. Yue opera is the major opera of the Guangdong Province because Guangdong's alternate name is Yue. Yu opera is the major opera of Henan Province because Henan is also called Yu.

LESSON 6 第六课
Idioms

AWAITING THE HARE UNDER THE TREE AND
SWORDPLAY AT THE ROOSTER'S CROW 守株待兔与闻鸡起舞

Idioms are fixed phrases that have formed over long periods of usage. An idiom usually consists of four characters. Idioms are vivid and terse, but also able to express rich meanings. The Chinese language has a long history, so its idioms are especially numerous. The majority of idioms have been used continuously since ancient times. They often have a fable or historical story behind them.

The idiom "awaiting the hare under the tree" represents a fable. During the Spring and Autumn period there was a farmer. One day he was working in the field. Suddenly, he saw a hare dash like an arrow, crash into a big tree, and die instantly. The farmer picked up the hare and said happily, "This is truly to get something without effort. I can have a delicious meal when I go back home." He went home, carrying the hare in hand, and thought with great satisfaction, "How lucky I was! Another hare might come tomorrow and I should not let an opportunity like this slip by." On the following day, when he came to the field he did not work, but only waited under the big tree. As a result, he got nothing after waiting for a whole day. However, he refused to give up. After that, he sat under the big tree every day waiting for hares to crash against the tree and die. He waited and waited, until the weeds in the field grew taller than the crops, and he did not see even one hare.

"Swordplay at the rooster's crow" tells a historical story. Zu Di and Liu Kun of the Jin dynasty shared a room and studied hard when they were young. One day, Zu Di heard the rooster crow while he was sleeping. He woke up Liu Kun and said, "The rooster is crowing. Let's get up and practice swordplay—how about that?" Having heard this, Liu Kun rolled out of bed. The two went into the yard and practiced swordplay under the moonlight. They did not put down their swords until the rosy clouds of dawn were full in the sky. After that, spring and autumn, summer and winter, they never stopped. After a long period of training, they finally became versatile men with literary talents and martial skills.

"Swordplay at the rooster's crow" shows a positive attitude toward life, but "awaiting the hare under the tree" depicts a negative lifestyle. There are many idioms both positive negative. Here are a few more examples: "Enhancing the eyes on a painted dragon" describes an effective effort, but "drawing a snake with feet" means to do superfluous things. Many idioms are also used to satirize and criticize. For example, one who "plays the zither to a cow" is a fool, one who acts as "the fox borrowing the tiger's fierceness" is a mean person, having "a honey mouth but a sword in the belly" indicates treachery, "to steal a bell with plugged ears" indicates self-deception, and "a mantis trying to stop a chariot with its arms" means overconfidence. Although the meanings of these idioms are clear at first reading, they also have stories behind them. Why don't you check them out online?

SOUTHBOUND CARRIAGE, NORTHBOUND TRACKS 南辕北辙

During the Warring States period, the King of Wei wanted to send troops to attack the State of Zhao. Minister Ji Liang was originally sent as an envoy to a neighboring state. Halfway there, he heard the news and immediately returned. He went to see the King of Wei in order to persuade him not to attack the State of Zhao.

Ji Liang told the King of Wei, "I saw a person on the way today who was in a carriage heading north but told me that he was heading toward the State of Chu. Chu is in the south, and I asked him why he was heading north when his destination is in the south. That person said, 'Don't worry. My horses are good; they run fast.' I reminded him that good horses were of no use; north is not the direction he should take to Chu. That person pointed to the big bag on the carriage and said, 'Don't worry. I have plenty of travel funds.' I told him again that travel funds were of no use and he would not get to Chu in this way. The person still said, 'Don't worry. My carriage driver is very good at driving.' That person is really confused. His directions were not right; even though his horses were especially fast, he carries a lot of travel funds, and his carriage driver is especially good at driving, none are of any use. The better these conditions are, the farther he will get from his destination."

Then Ji Liang touched upon the subject under discussion: "Your majesty wants to be the leader of different states; all your actions should be exemplary. If you attack other states just because your own state is big and your army is strong, you will not establish your power and popularity. This is just like the person who wanted to go to Chu. With 'southbound carriage, northbound tracks,' you will get farther and farther from your destination." The King of Wei was convinced by Ji Liang and decided to not attack the State of Zhao.

PROVERBS AND RIDDLES 谚语谜语

Proverbs are sayings that circulate among people; they often make the language lively and interesting and enhance the expressiveness of writing.

Some proverbs are single sentences, such as "All things prosper in a harmonious family," "There are no waves without wind," "Seeing once is better than hearing a hundred times," "Failure is the mother of success."

Some proverbs consist of two sentences. Some have four characters in each sentence, such as "Disease finds its way into the mouth; misfortunes come from the mouth" and "A thousand-mile journey begins with a single step." Some have five characters in each sentence, such as "At home you count on your parents; outside you rely on your friends" and "People go upward; water flows downward." Some have six characters in each sentence, such as "Heaven may produce unexpected winds and clouds; men may experience sudden happiness or calamity" and "Distant water will not put out a nearby fire; a distant relative is not as helpful as a nearby neighbor." Some have seven characters in each sentence, such as "The year's work is best begun in the spring and the day's work in the morning" and "A road must appear when the chariot approaches the mountain; the boat will naturally turn straight when it reaches the bridge's arch."

Riddles are a kind of language game. Guessing at riddles requires a certain amount of knowledge and is quite interesting. A riddle includes three parts:

mimian, mimu, and *midi. Mimian* poses a question; *midi* is the answer; and *mimu* is a clue to the scope of the answer. For example, 凤头虎尾 (phoenix's head and tiger's tail) is a *mimian,* "to guess a character" is the *mimu,* and the character 几 is the *midi,* because both the "head" of character 凤 and the "tail" of character 虎 are the character 几.

Character riddles are a type of riddle; that is, the answer is a character. Here are a few simple examples of character riddles. The answers to all of these riddles are characters; therefore, *mimu* has been omitted. The answers are in the parentheses, so you do not need to guess. However, you need to tell your professor why they are the answers.

LESSON 7 第七课

Holidays

CHANG'E FLYING TO THE MOON AND REUNION
ON THE MAGPIE BRIDGE 嫦娥奔月与鹊桥相会

There are many traditional holidays in China. The most important among them is of course Chinese New Year, also called the Spring Festival. Other important holidays include the Mid-Autumn Festival, the Dragon Boat Festival, and Tomb-Sweeping Day.

The Mid-Autumn Festival is a traditional holiday second only to the Spring Festival in importance. It is on the fifteenth day of the eighth lunar month. According to the lunar calendar, the seventh, eighth, and ninth months make up autumn. The fifteenth day of the eighth month is right in the middle of autumn, so it is called the Mid-Autumn Festival. The moon is full on the fifteenth day of each month of the lunar calendar. People consider the full moon a symbol of reunion, and take the Mid-Autumn Festival as a day of family reunion. On the night of the Mid-Autumn Festival, every family gets together to enjoy the moon and savor the moon cake.

On boxes of moon cakes there is often an image of a goddess. This is Chang'e, China's Moon Goddess. "Chang'e Flying to the Moon" is a famous mythological story. According to legend, after swallowing an immortal potion, Chang'e flew to heaven and became a goddess on the moon. When people look at the moon, they often say that the shadow on the moon is Chang'e's silhouette.

Looking up at the starry sky at the beginning of autumn, on the evening of the seventh day of the seventh lunar month, people will also talk about the story of the "Reunion on the Magpie Bridge."

There was a poor young man called Cowherd during the Zhou dynasty who was always with his old ox. It turned out that the old ox was originally a god in heaven who descended to the human world. One day, the old ox brought a beautiful girl to Cowherd. She was Weaver in heaven and had descended to the human world. Weaver saw that Cowherd was honest and sincere and fell in love with him. She further agreed to marry him. After the wedding, the man tilled the land and the woman wove cloth; they loved each other dearly. Weaver also gave birth to two lovely children—a boy and a girl.

They never knew, however, that the fact that Weaver secretly descended to the human world was known by the Queen Mother of the Western Heavens. She dispatched heavenly soldiers and generals to bring Weaver back to the palace. Cowherd put his two children in large bamboo baskets, shouldered them, and went to look for Weaver. With the help of the old ox, he flew up to the sky. When he saw Weaver ahead of him, he was noticed by the Queen Mother. She pulled a golden hairpin from her head and drew a line between Cowherd and Weaver. Immediately, the surging Milky Way appeared. Afterward, one of them was west of the river and the other east, and they could not meet. Their loyal love moved the magpies. On the evening of the seventh day of the seventh month, thousands and thousands of magpies flew to the river and connected themselves by biting each other's tails. Thus, they made a magpie bridge enabling Cowherd and Weaver to walk across it and meet. Queen Mother only allowed them to meet once a year on the magpie bridge—on the seventh day of the seventh month.

Later, when it came to be the seventh day of the seventh month, people looked up into the starry sky. Among the numerous stars of the autumn night, people saw two relatively large stars on the two sides of the Milky Way. These are the Cowherd Star (Vega) and Weaver Star (Altair). There are also two small stars with the Cowherd Star, and they are the son and daughter of the Cowherd and Weaver. Thus the Festival of the Seventh Night was created. Many people now consider this China's Valentine's Day.

A DROWNED POET 屈原沉江

The fifth day of the fifth lunar month is the Dragon Boat Festival; people eat *zongzi* and have dragon-boat regattas. It is said that all of these things commemorate poet Qu Yuan.

During the Warring States period, China was divided into seven states. The most powerful among them were the three states of Qin, Chu, and Qi. Qu Yuan was a courtier of Chu; he advocated political reform, allying with Qi, and resisting Qin. However, because of slander from a bad person, Qu Yuan was exiled to a remote region. During his exile, Qu Yuan wrote many poems expressing his innermost pain and his loyalty to Chu. In 278 BCE, the Qin army went south and attacked and destroyed the capital of Chu. On the fifth day of the fifth lunar month, Qu Yuan, filled with grief, committed suicide by drowning himself in the river.

Having heard that Qu Yuan had thrown himself in the river, people immediately rowed boats in hopes of taking him out of the water and saving him. This was later developed into the dragon-boat regatta. People also stuffed rice into bamboo tubes and put them in the river in order to feed Qu Yuan. This is the origin of *zongzi*.

CHINESE NEW YEAR TRADITIONS 春节习俗

The first day of the first lunar month is Chinese New Year, also called the Spring Festival; it is the grandest traditional holiday with the richest distinctive features.

On New Year's Eve, the whole family gets together to have New Year's Eve dinner. There are lavish dishes, and the names of the dishes often carry auspicious implications. For example, the steaming hotpot signifies prosperity. Another example is that fish is homophonic with "surplus" in Chinese, symbolizing "surplus every year." After the New Year's Eve dinner, children go into the yard to set off firecrackers and continue until after midnight, bidding farewell to the old and ushering in the new.

For breakfast on the first day of the year, people eat *niangao* (rice cakes), symbolizing "ascending higher every year." People also eat *tangyuan* (rice dumplings), implying family reunion. Afterward, the whole family goes to the homes of senior relatives and good friends to wish them a happy New Year; this is called *bainian*. At these kinds of visits, relatives of older generations often give children money, which is called *yasuiqian*, in red envelopes. In ancient times, New Year celebration activities did not end until the Lantern Festival on the fifteenth day of the first lunar month. Now they usually last for three days.

Spring Festival traditions have undergone many changes in modern days. On New Year's Eve, every family, while eating New Year's Eve dinner, watches the Spring Festival Gala performances on TV. With the development of science and technology, new forms of New Year greetings have appeared, such as greetings by telephone, text messages on cell phones, and online.

LESSON 8 第八课
Food and Drink

LI BAI GETS DRUNK AND WU SONG BEATS THE TIGER
太白醉酒和武松打虎

China has vast land, rich products, and a very long history; therefore, cuisines of different regions all have distinct features. For example, Sichuan cuisine is inclined to be hot and Shanghai dishes are relatively sweet. However, culinary arts from all regions require excellent color, smell, and taste. Dining should also be full of relish.

Therefore, one can often see dish names such as happy family, Dongpo's pork, and even dragon and phoenix.

China also produces good drink of all sorts, such as the hard liquor Maotai and Qingdao beer. There are many stories about wine drinking throughout the ages. Many poets felt that, after drinking, their imaginations would become active and they would have poetic inspiration.

The great poet Li Bai of the Tang dynasty has been called the immortal of poetry by later generations, but he called himself the immortal of wine. His friend Du Fu said, "Li Bai wrote a hundred poems after drinking a gallon of wine." Li Bai wrote a poem titled "Drinking Alone under the Moon." The four opening lines read, "A flask of wine among flowers, / I pour it alone without close friends. / I lift my cup to invite the bright moon, / Facing my shadow, we become three." This poem was widely read by later generations and "lifting a cup to invite the bright moon" also became a classic image of Li Bai. "Taibai Gets Drunk" was made the topic of many operas.

Like literary men, military officers of the ancient times also liked drinking. They felt that, after drinking, their courage would be doubled, and their martial arts skills would further increase. In the famous novel *The Water Margin* there is a hero named Wu Song who killed a tiger barehanded right after drinking.

Once Wu Song went back home to see his elder brother and passed by mountains called the Jingyang Ridge. There was a wine shop at the foot of the mountains. On the door hung a banner on which were inscribed five characters: "No ridge crossing after three bowls." Wu Song went into the shop and asked for two pounds of cooked beef. He drank three big bowls of wine in succession. While shouting, "Good wine!" Wu Song asked the shop owner to bring more. The shop owner said, "Didn't you see what was written on the banner? My wine is very strong. One will get drunk after drinking three bowls and will not be able to cross the Jingyang Ridge." However, Wu Song had an especially great capacity for drink; surprisingly, he drank eighteen bowls without a break.

When Wu Song finished drinking and was ready to leave the wine shop, the shop owner said that recently a big tiger appeared in the mountains. He urged Wu Song to wait for more people to climb the mountains together. However, Wu Song was not afraid of the tiger. He carried a wooden stick and drunkenly headed for the mountains. When he got to the mountaintops, suddenly there was a fierce gust of wind, and a great tiger pounced at Wu Song. Wu Song jumped aside swiftly and, as the fierce tiger turned, he lifted his wooden stick and aimed for the tiger's head with all of his strength. With a great snap, the stick hit a tree and broke in two. The tiger pounced upon Wu Song again. Wu Song threw away half of the stick. With his left hand, he grabbed the skin of the tiger's head and pressed the head to the ground. With his right hand, he lifted his iron hammer–like fist and beat the tiger's head without stopping. Not long afterward, he had beaten the tiger until it lay prostrate on the ground and could not move. From then on, Wu Song became a hero for beating the tiger; his martial arts fame spread far and wide.

BANQUET AT HONGMEN 鸿门酒宴

When one gives a banquet to entertain guests, the atmosphere should be very friendly. However, there are exceptions.

In the last years of the Qin dynasty, Liu Bang and Xiang Yu each fought the Qin army by themselves. Although Liu Bang's armed forces were not as strong as Xiang Yu's, he seized the capital, Xianyang, first. Xiang Yu's big army very soon rushed in and stationed itself in nearby Hongmen. Afraid of being destroyed by Xiang Yu, Liu Bang expressed his willingness to apologize. Xiang Yu thus invited Liu Bang to Hongmen for a banquet.

At the Hongmen banquet, although there was plenty of vintage wine and delicious food, the atmosphere was very tense. Fan Zeng, Xiang Yu's strategist, resolutely asked to kill Liu Bang. At the banquet he hinted to Xiang Yu again and again to give the order, but Xiang Yu hesitated. Fan Zeng then asked Xiang Zhuang, a general, to come to perform swordplay and liven the things up at the banquet, and to take the opportunity to kill Liu Bang. Zhang Liang, Liu Bang's strategist, and others protected Liu Bang and helped him escape. From then on, a Hongmen banquet became the synonym of a banquet with ill intentions behind it.

GONGBAO CHICKEN 宫保鸡丁

Gongbao chicken is a famous Sichuan dish, popular in China and overseas. In some restaurants it is written as Gongbao (宫爆) chicken, because some people think it is cooked using the quickfry (爆炒) method. Actually this is a misunderstanding, unclear as to the origin of Gongbao chicken.

The inventor of this dish was Ding Baozhen, a Sichuan governor during the Qing dynasty. Ding was very knowledgeable of culinary arts; he loved eating chicken and peanuts, and especially liked hot and spicy food. He created a delicious dish — use fresh and tender chicken cubes, tasty and crisp peanuts, plus red hot peppers; give it a quick fry in the pot; and there it is. Having eaten this dish, each and every guest praised it without cease. Later he was appointed junior guardian of the crown prince (太子少保) by the emperor, and people called him Ding Gongbao (丁宫保). This dish was thus called Gongbao chicken.

LESSON 9 第九章
Etiquette

STANDING IN THE SNOW AT THE TEACHER'S DOOR AND
THRICE VISITING THE THATCHED HOUSE 程门立雪与三顾茅庐

China has always been called a nation of etiquette. Etiquette was everywhere in traditional society. Chinese people's principles of etiquette include modesty toward others and respect for elders and superiors.

Revering teachers was an important part of traditional etiquette and virtue. Many stories regarding this have been handed down since ancient times.

Cheng Yi of the Song dynasty was a famous Confucian scholar and educator. He had a student named Yang Shi, who was already over forty years old and a fine scholar in his own right. One day, Yang Shi came for a lesson but at a time when the teacher was dozing at home. Yang Shi stood at the door, respectfully waiting for his teacher to awaken. After a little while, it began to snow and the flakes were as large as goose feathers. Yang Shi, however, continued to stand in the snow. Only when Cheng Yi woke from his nap did he find the "snowman" standing outside his house. Cheng Yi was deeply moved; thus, he taught and guided Yang Shi even more enthusiastically. Later, Yang Shi also became a famous Confucian scholar.

Respecting talent was a point of etiquette as well as an essential key to success for many leaders.

In the final years of the Han dynasty, the world was in chaos. Cao Cao, Liu Bei, and Sun Quan each controlled a territory. Liu Bei heard that Zhuge Liang, a hermit in the mountains, possessed great knowledge and talent. Therefore, he went with his sworn brothers Guan Yu and Zhang Fei to invite Zhuge Liang to leave the mountains and assist him. Unfortunately, Zhuge Liang was out that day, and Liu Bei could only return disappointed. Not long afterward, Liu Bei, Guan Yu, and Zhang Fei went a second time to extend the invitation to Zhuge Liang, and braved a fierce snowstorm. Unexpectedly, Zhuge Liang had left on an outing again. Liu Bei could only leave a letter, expressing his admiration for Zhuge Liang.

After some days, Liu Bei planned to go invite Zhuge Liang yet again. Guan Yu suggested that Zhuge Liang might have only an undeserved reputation instead of real talent and genuine knowledge, and that they should not go. Zhang Fei volunteered to go by himself; if Zhuge Liang would not come, Zhang Fei would tie him up with a rope and bring him. Liu Bei reproached Zhang Fei and went with the two of them to invite Zhuge Liang a third time. This time, Zhuge Liang was at home but was taking a nap. Liu Bei dared not bother him and stood waiting until Zhuge Liang woke up on his own. They then sat down together to talk.

Zhuge Liang saw that Liu Bei had aspirations to work for the country; his attitude was sincere, so he agreed with Liu Bei that he would leave the mountains. Later, Zhuge Liang assisted Liu Bei with great loyalty and helped him found the state of Shu. "Thrice Visiting the Thatched House" or "Thrice Inviting Zhuge Liang" has also become a tale of doing good deeds by seeking talent with sincerity.

A GENERAL'S APOLOGY 负荆请罪

During the Warring States period, in the state of Zhao there was a general called Lian Po and a courtier called Lin Xiangru. Lin Xiangru was still a low-ranking official when Lian Po was promoted to grand general long before. Later, Lin Xiangru was sent as an envoy to the powerful Qin and he defended the dignity and interests of Zhao with his wisdom and courage. He was therefore promoted to chief minister, a position even higher than that of Lian Po.

Lian Po was upset. He said to others, "I have military merit; however, Lin Xiangru, relying only on his mouth, now holds a higher position than I. When I come across Lin Xiangru, I will put him down." Having heard of this, Lin Xiangru exercised great caution and did his best to avoid Lian Po. On one occasion Lin Xiangru went out in his horse-drawn carriage; upon seeing Lian Po coming from afar, he hurriedly asked his driver to evade him.

Everyone around Lin Xiangru thought him timid. Lin Xiangru thus explained to them, "Just think: who is more formidable, the King of Qin or General Lian? I dared to reproach the King of Qin to his face at the Qin court; how could I be afraid of General Lian? The reason that Qin does not dare attack Zhao is the unity between General Lian and me, the chief minister. If General Lian and I do not get along, Qin will have an opportunity."

Having heard these words, Lian Po felt deeply guilty. Lian Po removed his upper clothing, carried a brambly stick on his back, and went to Lin Xiangru's home to ask for punishment. Thereafter, the two became lifelong friends.

THE FOUR BOOKS AND FIVE CLASSICS 四书五经

The Four Books and Five Classics is a general term referring to the nine Confucian classics, which ancient students were required to read.

The Five Classics refer to the *Classic of Poetry, Book of History, Book of Changes, Book of Rites,* and *Spring and Autumn Annals.* The *Classic of Poetry* is the earliest anthology of poetry in China. The *Book of History* is a collection of historical documents from antiquity. The *Book of Changes* explains the changes of yin and yang in the universe. The *Book of Rites* records and discusses the ritual system of the Zhou dynasty. *Spring and Autumn Annals* is a chronological history of the State of Lu.

The Four Books refer to the *Analects, Mencius,* the *Great Learning,* and *The*

Doctrine of the Mean. The *Analects* records the speeches and actions of Confucius and his disciples. *Mencius* records speeches and actions of Mencius and his disciples. The *Great Learning* and *The Doctrine of the Mean* were originally chapters of the *Book of Rites.* Zhu Xi, a scholar of the Southern Song dynasty, separated them into their own books and included them, with the *Analects* and *Mencius,* among the Four Books.

VOCABULARY INDEX 词汇索引

A

爱情	愛情	àiqíng	love	4.2
按		àn	to press, to push down	8.1
按照		ànzhào	according to	1.2

B

拔		bá	to draw (a sword)	1.1
白酒		báijiǔ	liquor, spirits	8.1
白首		báishǒu	white-haired, aged	1.1
柏		bǎi	cypress	2.1
百姓		bǎixìng	common people	5.1
拜		bài	to do obeisance, to bow, to kowtow	7.3
拜年		bàinián	to pay a New Year call	7.3
般		bān	sort, kind	8.1
扮		bàn	to disguise	4.2
半途		bàntú	halfway	6.2
邦		bāng	nation, state, country	9.1
榜样	榜樣	bǎngyàng	good example, role model	6.2
傍晚		bàngwǎn	dusk	2.1
包含		bāohán	to contain, to include	3.1
宝	寶	bǎo	treasure	1.1
宝贝	寶貝	bǎobèi	treasure	2.3
爆炒		bàochǎo	to quickfry	8.3
爆竹		bàozhú	firecracker	7.3
报晓	報曉	bàoxiǎo	to be a harbinger of dawn	6.1
暴躁		bàozào	hot tempered	5.1
碑		bēi	stele, tombstone	1.1
背		bēi	to carry on one's back	9.2
背		bèi	to recite from memory, to learn by heart	3.1
背		bèi	back (of the body)	3.2
悲愤	悲憤	bēifèn	grief	7.2
悲伤	悲傷	bēishāng	sad, mournful	4.1
被迫	被迫	bèipò	to be compelled	4.2
倍增	倍增	bèizēng	to double, to multiply	8.1

除夕		chúxī	New Year's Eve	3.3
处境	處境	chǔjìng	(unfavorable) situation	2.1
处在	處在	chùzài	to be (in a certain condition)	5.2
船		chuán	boat	3.1
船舱	船艙	chuáncāng	cabin	3.1
传家宝	傳家寶	chuánjiābǎo	heirloom	1.1
传世	傳世	chuánshì	to be handed down from generation to generation	2.1
创制	創制	chuàngzhì	to create	8.3
吹奏		chuīzòu	to play (wind instruments)	4.3
辞（职）	辭（職）	cí	to resign (from a job)	3.1
辞旧迎新	辭舊迎新	cíjiù yíngxīn	to bid farewell to the old and usher in the new	7.3
此外		cǐwài	besides, in addition	2.1
次于	次於	cìyú	second to	5.3
衰		cuī	to decline, to thin out	3.1
催		cuī	to push, to press, to hurry	4.2
脆		cuì	crisp, crunchy	8.3
存		cún	to exist	2.2

D

搭		dā	to put up, to build	7.1
答应	答應	dāying	to agree, to promise	4.2
打		dǎ	to guess (the answer to a riddle)	6.3
打败	打敗	dǎbài	to defeat (in war)	5.1
打扮		dǎbàn	to disguise, to make up	5.1
打盹儿	打盹兒	dǎdǔn	to doze off	9.1
打击	打擊	dǎjī	to strike	4.1
大臣		dàchén	minister, courtier	6.2
大惊失色	大驚失色	dàjīng shīsè	to go pale with fear	5.1
大师	大師	dàshī	master, grand master	5.2
大战	大戰	dàzhàn	great war, great battle	4.1
代名词	代名詞	dàimíngcí	another name, synonym	8.2
待人		dàirén	to treat people (in a certain way), to conduct oneself toward others	9.1
单单	單單	dāndān	only, alone	9.2
胆小	膽小	dǎnxiǎo	timid, cowardly	9.2
淡		dàn	light (color)	2.1

尔	爾	ěr	你	2.1
二胡		èrhú	*erhu*, a two-stringed Chinese fiddle	4.3

F

发令	發令	fālìng	to give an order	8.2
发明	發明	fāmíng	invention	2.3
发明者	發明者	fāmíngzhě	inventor	8.3
发生	發生	fāshēng	to happen, to take place	5.1
发源	發源	fāyuán	to originate	5.3
法术	法術	fǎshù	black magic, supernatural feats	5.1
翻		fān	to cross, to get over, to climb over	2.2
翻身		fānshēn	to turn over	6.1
繁		fán	many, numerous	7.1
反而		fǎn'ér	on the contrary, instead	6.2
返回		fǎnhuí	to return	6.2
烦恼	煩惱	fánnǎo	vexation, worry	3.3
范围	範圍	fànwéi	scope, range	6.3
方		fāng	才	1.1
方面		fāngmiàn	respect, aspect	9.1
方向		fāngxiàng	direction	6.2
访	訪	fǎng	to visit	5.2
仿佛	仿佛	fǎngfú	好像, as if	4.1
放		fàng	to set off (a firecracker)	7.3
放过	放過	fàngguò	to let slip by	6.1
放牛		fàngniú	to herd water buffalo	2.1
放松	放鬆	fàngsōng	to loosen	2.1
诽谤	誹謗	fěibàng	slander	7.2
费	費	fèi	to cost, to spend	6.1
分别		fēnbié	to part	4.2
吩咐		fēnfu	to tell, to instruct, to order	9.2
坟墓	墳墓	fénmù	grave, tomb	4.1
封		fēng	to confer (a title, territory, etc) upon, to appoint	8.3
枫	楓	fēng	maple	3.1
风趣	風趣	fēngqù	humorous	6.3
丰盛	豐盛	fēngshèng	lavish, sumptuous	7.3
讽刺	諷刺	fěngcì	to satirize	6.1

解脱	解脫	jiětuō	to extricate	3.3
斤		jīn	unit of weight (equal to half a kilogram)	8.1
金钗		jīnchāi	golden hairpin	7.1
金文		jīnwén	inscriptions on bronze	1.1
仅	僅	jǐn	只, only, merely	5.3
尽量	儘量	jǐnliàng	to the best of one's ability, as far as possible	9.2
谨慎	謹慎	jǐnshèn	prudent, careful, cautious	5.1
尽	盡	jìn	exhausted	1.2
近代		jìndài	modern times	5.2
晶		jīng	brilliant, glittering	6.3
荆		jīng	bramble, thorn	9.2
经典	經典	jīngdiǎn	classical	4.1
经过	經過	jīngguò	having gone through, after	6.1
惊动	驚動	jīngdòng	to alarm, to startle	9.1
惊心动魄	驚心動魄	jīngxīn dòngpò	stirring, fiercely intense	4.1
精美		jīngměi	exquisite	2.3
精神		jīngshén	spirit	2.1
景象		jǐngxiàng	scenery, sight	3.1
竟		jìng	unexpectedly, surprisingly	8.1
竟然		jìngrán	surprisingly	1.1
揪		jiū	to hold tight, to grab	8.1
究竟		jiūjìng	actually, after all	1.2
酒量		jiǔliàng	capacity for drink	8.1
居住		jūzhù	to live	5.1
举	舉	jǔ	to lift	3.1
举办	舉辦	jǔbàn	to hold, to sponsor (an event, etc.)	3.3
举例子	舉例子	jǔlìzi	to give examples	6.1
聚		jù	to assemble, to gather	1.2
据	據	jù	to occupy, to hold	9.1
俱		jù	都	8.1
巨大		jùdà	tremendous, enormous	5.2
聚会	聚會	jùhuì	gathering, party	1.1
聚精会神	聚精會神	jùjīng huìshén	to focus one's attention on, to be engrossed in	1.2
剧目	劇目	jùmù	list of plays or operas	5.1
剧团	劇團	jùtuán	theatrical company, troupe	5.2

老大		lǎodà	年老	3.1
礼貌	禮貌	lǐmào	courtesy, manners	3.2
礼仪	禮儀	lǐyí	ceremony and propriety, etiquette	9.1
利		lì	profit	1.1
厉害	屬害	lìhài	formidable	9.2
立刻		lìkè	immediately	6.2
隶书	隸書	lìshū	clerical script	1.1
例外		lìwài	exception	8.2
利益		lìyì	interest, benefit	9.2
利诱	利誘	lìyòu	to tempt with material gain	1.1
联	聯	lián	to ally	7.2
连接	連接	liánjiē	to join, to link	7.1
连连	連連	liánlián	again and again	3.2
脸谱	臉譜	liǎnpǔ	facial design (in Beijing opera)	5.1
梁	樑	liáng	roof beam	2.2
梁上君子	樑上君子	liángshàng jūnzǐ	thief	2.2
裂		liè	to split, to crack	4.2
铃	鈴	líng	bell	6.1
灵感	靈感	línggǎn	inspiration	8.1
领导	領導	lǐngdǎo	to lead	4.1
领袖	領袖	lǐngxiù	leader	6.2
流传	流傳	liúchuán	to circulate, to hand down	6.3
流放		liúfàng	exile	7.2
龙凤呈祥	龍鳳呈祥	lóngfèng chéngxiáng	prosperity brought by the dragon and the phoenix, extremely good fortune	8.1
隆重	隆重	lóngzhòng	grand, ceremonious	7.3
驴	驢	lú	donkey	3.2
旅途		lǚtú	journey, trip	3.1
论述	論述	lùnshù	to discuss, to explicate	9.3
箩筐	籮筐	luókuāng	large bamboo or wicker basket	7.1
落		luò	to fall, to drop	3.1

M

马蹄	馬蹄	mǎtí	horse's hoof	4.1
满	滿	mǎn	full	2.1
满腔		mǎnqiāng	(with one's heart) filled with, full of	7.2
满意	滿意	mǎnyì	pleased, satisfied	3.2

泥浆		níjiāng	slop, soft mud	1.1
年糕		niángāo	New Year cake (made of glutinous rice flour)	7.3
年龄	年齡	niánlíng	age	3.1
年夜饭	年夜飯	niányèfàn	New Year's Eve dinner	7.3
娘家		niángjiā	home of a married woman's parents	4.3
娘子		niángzi	lady, wife (in early vernacular)	5.1
浓	濃	nóng	thick, dense, heavy	2.3
农夫	農夫	nóngfū	peasant, farmer	6.1
农历	農曆	nónglì	Chinese lunar calendar	3.3
努力		nǔlì	effort	6.1

O

偶		ǒu	incidental, accidental, occasional	3.1

P

趴		pā	to lie prostrate	8.1
派		pài	to send, to assign, to appoint	5.1
叛乱	叛亂	pànluàn	rebellion	1.1
胖		pàng	fat, plump	6.3
袍		páo	robe, gown	5.1
烹饪	烹飪	pēngrèn	cuisine, culinary arts	8.1
碰见	碰見	pèngjiàn	to meet unexpectedly, to run or bump into	9.2
碰巧		pèngqiǎo	coincidentally	3.2
披		pī	to drape over one's shoulders	2.2
皮		pí	skin	8.1
琵琶		pípá	*pipa*, a plucked stringed instrument with a fretted fingerboard	4.1
偏		piān	to incline, to lean to one side	8.1
贫苦	貧苦	pínkǔ	poor, poverty stricken	2.1
品尝	品嘗	pǐncháng	to taste, to savor, to sample	7.1
品格		pǐngé	moral character	2.1
凭	憑	píng	to rely on, to depend on	9.2
平安		píng'ān	safe and sound	3.3
破		pò	broken	2.1
扑	撲	pū	to pounce, to dash at	8.1

泉		quán	spring (water)	4.3
全才		quáncái	person of many talents	6.1
拳头	拳頭	quántóu	fist	8.1
犬		quǎn	狗, dog	1.2
劝	勸	quàn	to persuade, to urge	1.1
鹊	鵲	què	magpie	7.1

R

热气腾腾	熱氣騰騰	rèqì téngténg	steaming hot	7.3
人才		réncái	talent, person of ability	9.1
人格		réngé	personality, moral quality	1.1
人士		rénshì	people	3.3
忍让	忍讓	rěnràng	to exercise forbearance	9.2
任		rèn	to let one act at will, no matter (how, what, etc.)	2.1
扔掉		rēngdiào	to throw away	8.1
如		rú	像	1.1
儒家		rújiā	Confucian	9.1
入睡		rùshuì	to fall asleep	3.1
若		ruò	像	1.1

S

塞		sāi	to fill, to stuff	7.2
散发	散發	sànfā	to scatter, to disperse	2.1
扫帚	掃帚	sàozhǒu	broom	1.1
色彩		sècǎi	color	2.1
僧		sēng	Buddhist monk	3.2
傻瓜		shǎguā	fool, idiot	6.1
伤感	傷感	shānggǎn	sorrow	3.1
伤心	傷心	shāngxīn	sad, brokenhearted	4.2
上古		shànggǔ	ancient times, antiquity	9.3
少保		shàobǎo	junior guardian	8.3
少小		shàoxiǎo	at an early age	3.1
折		shé	to break, to snap	8.1
蛇	蛇	shé	snake	5.1
舍（得）		shěde	to be ready to part with or give up	4.2
设宴	設宴	shèyàn	to give a banquet	8.2
身后	身後	shēnhòu	after one's death	1.1

说服	說服	shuōfú	to persuade, to convince	6.2
说明	說明	shuōmíng	to explain, to illustrate	2.1
思考		sīkǎo	to think deeply, to ponder	3.2
思念		sīniàn	to think of, to miss	3.1
私自		sīzì	secretly, without permission	7.1
死讯	死訊	sǐxùn	news of somebody's death	7.2
松		sōng	pine	2.1
松		sōng	to loosen, to relax, to relieve	5.1
随手	隨手	suíshǒu	conveniently, without extra trouble	1.2
碎		suì	broken	4.1
损	損	sǔn	to damage	2.2
唢呐		suǒnà	*suona*, a woodwind horn	4.3

T

塔		tǎ	pagoda	1.1
台	臺	tái	terrace, stage	4.1
态度	態度	tàidù	attitude	6.1
太子		tàizǐ	crown prince	8.3
弹拨	彈撥	tánbō	to pluck	4.1
叹	嘆	tàn	to sigh	1.2
探望		tànwàng	to pay a visit	8.1
螳		táng	mantis	6.1
特色		tèsè	distinctive feature	5.1
特异	特異	tèyì	peculiar, distinctive	5.1
啼		tí	(of birds) to caw, to sing	3.1
提		tí	to carry (in hand with arm hanging down)	6.1
提升		tíshēng	to promote	9.2
提醒		tíxǐng	to remind	6.2
题材	題材	tícái	subject, topic	8.1
题诗	題詩	tíshī	to inscribe a poem (on a painting, etc.)	2.1
体现		tǐxiàn	manifestation, reflection, expression	1.1
替		tì	为	9.1
天兵天将	天兵天將	tiānbīng tiānjiāng	soldiers and generals from heaven	7.1
天下		tiānxià	under the heavens; world, country	1.1
挑		tiāo	to carry on the shoulder with a pole	7.1
条件	條件	tiáojiàn	condition, circumstance	6.2
铁锤	鐵錘	tiěchuí	iron hammer	8.1

停		tíng	to stop, to cease, to halt	4.2
挺立		tǐnglì	to stand upright	2.1
统一	統一	tóngyī	to unify	1.3
统称	統稱	tǒngchēng	collective name, general designation	2.3
头	頭	tóu	measure word for oxen, donkeys, etc.	3.2
徒		tú	in vain, to no avail	9.1
徒手		túshǒu	barehanded, unarmed	8.1
徒有虚名		túyǒu xūmíng	with undeserved reputation, nominal, in name only	9.1
图章	圖章	túzhāng	seal, stamp	1.1
兔		tù	hare, rabbit	6.1
团	團	tuán	round, circular	7.1
团聚	團聚	tuánjù	reunion	7.1
推		tuī	to push	3.2
脱		tuō	to take off, to undress	9.2

W

完美		wánměi	perfect	2.1
网	網	wǎng	World Wide Web, the internet	6.1
往往		wǎngwǎng	常常	3.1
威		wēi	prowess, might	6.1
威名	威名	wēimíng	fame (won by military/martial exploits)	8.1
威信		wēixìn	prestige, power, popularity	6.2
围	圍	weí	to surround	1.1
维护	維護	wéihù	to safeguard, to preserve, to defend	9.2
惟有		wéiyǒu	只有	1.2
为止	為止	weízhǐ	until, up to	3.3
尾		wěi	tail	2.2
畏		wèi	怕	2.1
未必		wèibì	not necessarily	9.1
文		wén	measure word for ancient coins	2.2
文房		wénfáng	书房	2.3
文件		wénjiàn	documents	9.3
文具		wénjù	stationery	2.3
文人		wénrén	man of letters, scholar	2.3
握手		wòshǒu	to shake hands	5.2
乌	烏	wū	crow	3.1
吾		wú	我	1.2

舞剑	舞劍	wǔjiàn	to perform swordplay	8.2
武将	武將	wǔjiàng	military officer, general	8.1
武术	武術	wǔshù	martial arts	5.1
武艺	武藝	wǔyì	martial arts skills	8.1
午夜		wǔyè	midnight	7.3
误解	誤解	wùjiě	to misunderstand	8.3

X

悉心		xīxīn	wholehearted	9.1
吸引		xīyǐn	to attract	2.1
习俗	習俗	xísú	custom	7.3
喜酒		xǐjiǔ	wedding banquet	4.3
喜庆	喜慶	xǐqìng	jubilant and festive	4.3
喜鹊	喜鵲	xǐquè	magpie	7.1
喜悦	喜悅	xǐyuè	joy	3.1
戏剧	戲劇	xìjù	drama	5.1
戏曲	戲曲	xìqǔ	traditional opera	5.3
细雨	細雨	xìyǔ	fine rain	2.2
下达	下達	xiàdá	to issue (an order)	5.1
下凡		xiàfán	(of gods or immortals) to descend to the world	7.1
下令	下令	xiàlìng	to give orders	5.1
仙		xiān	celestial being, immortal	8.1
仙女		xiānnǚ	celestial lady, goddess	7.1
鲜嫩	鮮嫩	xiānnèn	fresh and tender	8.3
鲜艳	鮮豔	xiānyàn	brightly colored	2.1
弦		xián	string (on an instrument)	4.3
贤	賢	xián	virtuous and capable, worthy	9.1
闲游	閒遊	xiányóu	to stroll	9.1
香		xiāng	fragrance	2.1
相伴		xiāngbàn	to accompany each other	7.1
相传	相傳	xiāngchuán	according to legend	7.1
相当	相當	xiāngdāng	quite, fairly, rather	9.1
相会	相會	xiānghuì	to meet each other	7.1
乡音	鄉音	xiāngyīn	accent of one's native place	3.1
相遇		xiāngyù	to meet, to come across	4.1
相貌	相貌	xiàngmào	facial features, looks, appearance	5.1
降	降	xiáng	to surrender	1.1
祥		xiáng	luck, auspiciousness	8.1

疑		yí	to suspect	3.1
疑惑	疑惑	yíhuò	to feel puzzled, to be doubtful	5.1
遗憾	遺憾	yíhàn	to regret	5.2
仪式	儀式	yíshì	ceremony, rite	4.3
以		yǐ	用	4.1
以		yǐ	because of	9.2
阴阳	陰陽	yīnyáng	yin and yang, opposite forces in nature	9.3
阴影	陰影	yīnyǐng	shadow	7.1
吟		yín	to chant (poems)	2.2
隐居	隱居	yǐnjū	to retire from public life and live in seclusion, to be a hermit	9.1
饮食	飲食	yǐnshí	food and drink, diet	8.1
影		yǐng	shadow	2.2
映		yìng	to reflect, to show through	2.2
英雄		yīngxióng	hero	8.1
英勇		yīngyǒng	heroic, brave	1.1
应用	應用	yīngyòng	to use, to apply	4.3
影响深远	影響深遠	yǐngxiǎng shēnyuǎn	profound influence	1.3
勇猛		yǒngměng	valorous and powerful	5.1
勇气	勇氣	yǒngqì	courage	8.1
悠久		yōujiǔ	long, age-old	6.1
优雅	優雅	yōuyǎ	elegant, graceful	4.1
由		yóu	by (somebody)	9.1
由于……关系	由於……關係	yóuyú … guānxì	because of, due to	5.2
犹豫不决	猶豫不決	yóuyù bùjué	to hesitate, to remain undecided	8.2
有效		yǒuxiào	effective	6.1
友谊	友誼	yǒuyì	friendship	5.2
诱	誘	yòu	to tempt	1.1
于		yú	在	4.3
于是	於是	yúshì	therefore, as a result	9.2
余	餘	yú	surplus, remainder	7.3
渔火	漁火	yúhuǒ	fishing light	3.1

正月		zhēngyuè	first month of the lunar year	7.3
正反		zhèngfǎn	positive and negative, both sides	6.1
政治		zhèngzhì	politics, political affairs	7.2
之		zhī	的	1.1
之间	之間	zhījiān	between, among	7.1
支		zhī	measure word for army units, etc.	1.1
织	織	zhī	to weave	7.1
植物		zhíwù	plant, vegetable	2.1
直至		zhízhì	until, up to	4.1
止		zhǐ	stop, end	3.3
指		zhǐ	to refer to	9.3
志		zhì	will, aspiration, ambition	9.1
制度		zhìdù	rules, regulations, system	1.3
忠诚	忠誠	zhōngchéng	loyal, faithful	5.1
忠厚		zhōnghòu	honest and sincere	7.1
忠心耿耿		zhōngxīn gěnggěng	loyal and devoted	9.1
忠贞	忠貞	zhōngzhēn	loyal and staunch	7.1
终身	終身	zhōngshēn	lifelong	3.1
终于	終于	zhōngyú	finally, eventually	1.2
种类	種類	zhǒnglèi	kind, category	2.1
株		zhū	measure word for trees and plants	2.1
株		zhū	trunk, stump	6.1
逐渐	逐漸	zhújiàn	gradually	7.2
主张	主張	zhǔzhāng	to advocate	7.2
主体	主體	zhǔtǐ	subject, perceiver	3.1
祝贺	祝賀	zhùhè	to congratulate	7.3
著名		zhùmíng	famous	1.1
助手		zhùshǒu	assistant	5.1
助兴	助興	zhùxìng	to add to the fun, to liven things up	8.2
驻扎	駐紮	zhùzhā	(of troops) to be stationed	8.2
抓		zhuā	to catch, to arrest	7.1
传	傳	zhuàn	biography, story	5.1
篆书	篆書	zhuànshū	seal script	1.1
庄稼	莊稼	zhuāngjia	crops	6.1
撞		zhuàng	to bump against, to crash	6.1
酌		zhuó	to pour wine, to drink	8.1
卓越		zhuóyuè	outstanding, excellent	1.1

自		zì	从	5.1
字		zì	style name	2.1
字体	字體	zìtǐ	style of calligraphy	2.3
综合	綜合	zōnghé	comprehensive, composite	5.1
总督	總督	zǒngdū	governor general	8.3
总集	總集	zǒngjí	anthology	9.3
总统	總統	zǒngtǒng	president (of a state)	5.2
醉醺醺		zuìxūnxūn	drunkenly	8.1
尊严	尊嚴	zūnyán	dignity, integrity, honor	9.2
尊重		zūnzhòng	to respect	9.1
座		zuò	measure word for houses, bridges, etc.	7.1
作品		zuòpǐn	works (of art and literature)	1.1
作用		zuòyòng	role, function	4.3
作战	作戰	zuòzhàn	to fight, to fight a battle	1.1
做人		zuòrén	to be a person of integrity	2.2

PROPER NAMES INDEX 专名索引

B

| 白娘子 | | Bái Niángzi | personal name | 5.1 |
| 伯牙 | | Bóyá | a legendary *qin* master | 4.1 |

C

曹操		Cáo Cāo	king of Wei (r. 208–220)	9.1
长安	長安	Cháng'ān	Tang capital, present-day Xi'an 西安	3.2
嫦娥		Cháng'é	Goddess of the Moon	7.1
程颐	程頤	Chéng Yí	Neo-Confucian scholar (1033–1107)	9.1
楚		Chǔ	name of Xiang Yu's army	4.1
春秋		Chūnqiū	Spring and Autumn period (722–481 BCE)	4.1

D

丁宝桢	丁寶楨	Dīng Bǎozhēn	Qing governor (1820–1886)	8.3
东坡	東坡	Dōngpō	Su Shi (also known as Su Dongpo, 1037–1101), Song poet, calligrapher, and statesman	8.1
杜甫		Dù Fǔ	Tang poet (712–770)	8.1
端午节	端午節	Duānwǔ jié	Dragon Boat Festival	7.1

F

| 法海 | | Fǎhǎi | Buddhist monk | 5.1 |
| 范增 | 范增 | Fàn Zēng | strategist of Xiang Yu's | 8.2 |

G

姑苏	姑蘇	Gūsū	ancient name for Suzhou City	3.1
关羽	關羽	Guān Yǔ	general of Liu Bei's (d. 220)	9.1
广东	廣東	Guǎngdōng	Guangdong Province	5.3

H

韩愈	韓愈	Hán Yù	Tang poet (768–825)	3.2
寒山寺		Hánshān sì	Cold Mountain Temple in Suzhou	3.1
汉朝	漢朝	Hàncháo	Han dynasty (202 BCE–220 CE)	1.1

银河		Yínhé	Milky Way	7.1
豫		Yù	alternative name for Henan	5.3
元朝		Yuáncháo	Yuan dynasty (1271–1368)	1.3
元宵节	元宵節	Yuánxiāo jié	Lantern Festival	7.3
粤		Yuè	alternative name for Guangdong	5.3

Z

战国	戰國	Zhànguó	Warring States period (475–221 BCE)	6.2
张飞	張飛	Zhāng Fēi	general of Liu Bei's (d. 221)	9.1
张继	張繼	Zhāng Jì	Tang poet (d. 779)	3.1
张良	張良	Zhāng Liáng	strategist of Liu Bang's	8.2
赵国	趙國	Zhàoguó	State of Zhao (403–222 BCE)	6.2
浙江		Zhèjiāng	Zhejiang Province	1.1
镇江	鎮江	Zhènjiāng	city in Jiangsu Province	5.1
郑燮	鄭燮	Zhèng Xiè	Qing painter (1693–1765)	2.1
织女	織女	Zhīnǚ	Weaver	7.1
织女星	織女星	Zhīnǚ xīng	Vega (star)	7.1
钟子期	鍾子期	Zhōng Zǐqī	personal name	4.1
中秋节	中秋節	Zhōngqiūjié	Mid-Autumn Festival, Moon Festival	7.1
中庸		Zhōngyōng	*The Doctrine of the Mean*	9.3
周朝		Zhōucháo	Zhou dynasty (1046–256 BCE)	1.1
竺		Zhú	surname	6.3
朱熹		Zhū Xī	Confucian thinker and educator (1130–1200)	9.3
祝英台		Zhù Yīngtái	personal name	4.2
诸葛亮	諸葛亮	Zhūgě Liàng	Shu strategist (181–234)	5.1
卓别林		Zhuóbiélín	Charlie Chaplin (1889–1977)	5.2
祖逖	祖逖	Zǔ Tì	Jin general (266–321)	6.1